Cambridge Elements ☰

Elements in Musical Theatre
edited by
William A. Everett
University of Missouri–Kansas City

KICKSTARTING ITALIAN OPERA IN THE ANDES

The 1840s and the First Opera Companies

José Manuel Izquierdo König
Pontificia Catholic University of Chile

Shaftesbury Road, Cambridge CB2 8EA, United Kingdom

One Liberty Plaza, 20th Floor, New York, NY 10006, USA

477 Williamstown Road, Port Melbourne, VIC 3207, Australia

314–321, 3rd Floor, Plot 3, Splendor Forum, Jasola District Centre,
New Delhi – 110025, India

103 Penang Road, #05–06/07, Visioncrest Commercial, Singapore 238467

Cambridge University Press is part of Cambridge University Press & Assessment,
a department of the University of Cambridge.

We share the University's mission to contribute to society through the pursuit of
education, learning and research at the highest international levels of excellence.

www.cambridge.org
Information on this title: www.cambridge.org/9781009223058

DOI: 10.1017/9781009223027

First published 2023

A catalogue record for this publication is available from the British Library.

ISBN 978-1-009-22305-8 Paperback
ISSN 2631-6528 (online)
ISSN 2631-651X (print)

Kickstarting Italian Opera in the Andes

The 1840s and the First Opera Companies

Elements in Musical Theatre

DOI: 10.1017/9781009223027
First published online: January 2023

José Manuel Izquierdo König
Pontificia Universidad Católica de Chile

Author for correspondence: José Manuel Izquierdo König, juizquie@uc.cl

Abstract: During the nineteenth century, Italian opera became truly transatlantic and its rapid expansion is one of the most exciting new areas of study in music and the performing arts. Beyond the Atlantic coasts, opera searched for new spaces to expand its reach. This Element discusses Italian opera in the Andean countries of Chile, Peru, Ecuador and Bolivia during the 1840s and focuses on opera as a product that both challenged and was challenged in the Andes by other forms of performing arts, behaviours, technologies, material realities and business models.

This Element also has a video abstract:
www.cambridge.org/Musical Theatre_Konig_abstract

Keywords: Italian opera, Andean region, transatlantic, global history, impresario

ISBNs: 9781009223058 (PB), 9781009223027 (OC)
ISSNs: 2631-6528 (online), 2631-651X (print)

Contents

Introduction

On 30 July 1840, the small brig *Carmen* arrived in Callao, the old harbour of Lima. Eleven artists, most of them Italian and one Cuban arrived on the ship from Havana via the ports of Panama, with the dream of establishing an opera company in the capital of Peru. In Peru, however, no one expected their arrival: the news came with Cuban newspapers aboard that same ship.[1] As far as we know, Italian opera had been performed in Peru before, including by two Italian singers in 1812, as well as by a small travelling company in 1831. This time was different: the singers travelled from Cuba, a well-known operatic centre, and the troupe was a professional group, with at least one prominent Italian star (Clorinda Corradi), and her husband, a conductor-impresario willing to develop a permanent operatic scene (Raffaele Pantanelli). As one account put it eight years later, in the Andes the arrival of the Pantanelli company, as it would be known, kick-started a period of 'pleasure in which our knowledge and passion for opera became generalised'.[2]

There were a few false starts. The first negotiations in August 1840 were not easy; there was pressure from local dramatic actors and politicians to prioritize Peruvian- and Spanish-speaking productions over a foreign company. Some feared that history would repeat itself: there would be some performances, for which people would pay a lot of money, and then when the troupe left, local artists would be in the difficult position of resuming their work under unfair comparison.[3] To appease the rabble-rousers, the contract between the managers of the local theatre, and Pantanelli, the impresario, was published in the main local newspaper, *El Comercio*.[4]

The company performed for the first time on September 2, and the two main newspapers of Lima, *El Comercio* and *El Amigo del Pueblo*, dedicated a full page each to discuss their performance of Bellini's *I Capuleti,* sold locally as *Romeo y Julieta*: 'The opera exceeded everything we had hope for.'[5] The Pantanelli company performed in Lima until 1844, when the singers, reinforced with new voices in 1842 and 1843, moved to Chile to continue performing in other Andean cities. During the 1840s members of the Pantanelli company performed operas – often for the first time – in almost all major Andean cities, in countries like Chile, Peru, Ecuador and Bolivia: Guayaquil, Arequipa, Lambayeque, La Paz, Talca and Copiapo. The theatres that were built at the time of their performances, and the local, regional and transatlantic networks they developed, set the groundwork for operatic, drama and zarzuela

---

https://storymaps.arcgis.com/stories/1706a9a38fb24beca2ea526e07b7a0ff
Readers can follow the story of the opera companies working in the Andes during the 1840s through this ArcGIS Storymap, specially prepared as an accompaniment to this Element.
[1] *El Comercio*, Lima, 10 August 1840.   [2] *El Comercio*, Lima, 25 April 1848.
[3] *El Amigo del Pueblo*, Lima, 11 August 1840.   [4] *El Comercio*, Lima, 8 August 1840.
[5] *El Amigo del Pueblo*, Lima, 3 September 1840.

performances well into the twentieth century. Even more, many of those singers stayed in the Andes for life, becoming key figures in the creation of local and regional cultural scenes, well beyond the frameworks of Italian opera performances.

This Element is about that early process of reception of Italian opera and Italian opera artists in the Andes. It is a key period, when Italian opera, its repertoire, artists and modes of production, were becoming global, as it has been recognized by recent scholarship.[6] A focus on Latin America and specific regions of Latin America, as Paulo Kühl and Axel Körner have recently suggested, might be particularly important to opera and music theatre scholarship today, since it 'allows for a critical assessment of the postcolonial condition of opera production' in new nations that 'continued to maintain close relations with Europe'.[7] The question, of course, is what does a critical assessment of the postcolonial condition of opera production look like. As a borderline, a 'frontier' of operatic expansion in the age of early imperialism, Italian opera in the Andes during the 1840s allows us to focus on opera not as a granted and accepted cultural form. Italian opera was not imposed, and its global character was not entirely obvious. It had to gain a place, becoming a force for conflict, a product both challenging and being challenged by other forms of performing arts, cultural businesses and entertainments.

There has been much research and interest in operatic reception outside Europe in the early twenty-first century. In part, the interest in operatic reception extends the idea that opera is, by its very nature, 'a historically situated synthesis of means and artistic expressions that can mediate and transcend temporal, geographical and social boundaries'.[8] In the words of Suzanne Aspden, 'opera's cultural mobility has allowed it to be used to negotiate, heighten, and at times transcend boundaries of identity', a process that was just as potent in Europe as when 'opera was exported to other territories, as a marker in various ways of European civilization and power'.[9] It is not only that opera became tremendously important for Latin American politics and culture. Latin America became tremendously important for operatic history during the nineteenth

---

[6] Benjamin Walton, 'Italian Operatic Fantasies in Latin America', *Journal of Modern Italian Studies* 17 (2012), 460–71; Suzanne Aspden (ed.), *Operatic Geographies: The Place of Opera and the Opera House* (University of Chicago Press, 2019); Mark Everist, *The Empire at the Opéra: Theatre, Power and Music in Second Empire Paris* (Cambridge University Press, 2021). Also, coming from theatre studies, Christopher Balme, *The Globalization of Theatre 1870–1930: Theatrical Networks of Maurice E. Bandmann* (Cambridge University Press, 2019).

[7] Paulo Kühl and Axel Körner, *Italian Opera in Global and Transnational Perspective: Reimagining Italianità in the Long Nineteenth Century* (Cambridge University Press, 2022), 8.

[8] Roberta Montemorra, *Operatic Migrations: Transforming Works and Crossing Boundaries* (Routledge, 2017).

[9] Aspden, *Operatic Geographies*, 9.

century; in particular for companies that could work, for example, in Cuba, Rio de Janeiro and/or Buenos Aires, benefitting from a summer season during the European winter, working between Italian seasons.[10]

Recent studies on the early reception of opera in the broader American and Caribbean region have shown that there is much to be learned from the period.[11] My focus is, however, more specifically on the Andes and the South Pacific region of the Americas. In terms of operatic reception, the Andes has been much less explored and researched than Brazil, the United States, Mexico or Argentina, countries well connected to the Atlantic and, thus, to Europe and an established notion of 'transatlantic' culture. The Andes serves as the back-bone of South America, crossing the continent in a north–south Axis. It separates nations bordering the Atlantic from those connected to the Pacific, including Colombia, Ecuador, Peru, Bolivia and Chile. While Colombia, like Venezuela, could be considered part of the Andes, it is not included in my framework here, since it has been traditionally dependent on the Caribbean, because of the position of its main port. For most of the nineteenth century, its operatic connections were more Caribbean than Andean.[12]

Ecuador, Peru, Bolivia and Chile, however, are firmly defined by the Andes. For those interested in migrating to the Andes during the nineteenth century, the region presented a series of challenges and opportunities that are slightly different to those in other parts of the Americas. Travelling to the Andes from the Atlantic was only possible through three different routes, all of them dangerous: through Panama's ports and then alongside the Pacific coast, on horseback through the Argentinean Pampas, or by crossing the dangerous Cape Horn alongside Tierra del Fuego. Only in the 1840s did steamship travel allow for regular connections between these countries, bypassing the difficult and arid landscapes that cover the coasts of Peru and the north of Chile, as well enormous distances involved: steamers connected a new maritime network of port cities

---

[10] Ditlev Rindom, 'Bygone Modernity: Re-imagining Italian Opera in Milan, New York and Buenos Aires, 1887–1914', unpublished PhD thesis, University of Cambridge (2019); Matteo Paoletti, *A Huge Revolution of Theatrical Commerce: Walter Mocchi and the Italian Musical Theatre Business in South America* (Cambridge University Press, 2020). See also from Matteo Paoletti, 'La red de empresarios europeos en Buenos Aires (1880–1925): Algunas consideraciones preliminares', *Revista Argentina de Musicología* 21 (2020), 51–76.

[11] Pierpaolo Polzonetti, *Italian Opera in the Age of the American Revolution* (Cambridge University Press, 2011); Charlotte Bentley, 'Resituating Transatlantic Opera: The Case of the Théâtre d'Orléans, New Orleans, 1819–1859', unpublished PhD thesis, University of Cambridge (2017); Francesco Milella, 'Italian Opera and Creole Identities: Manuel García in Independent Mexico (1826–1829)', in Paulo Kühl and Axel Körner (eds.), *Italian Opera in Global and Transnational Perspective: Reimagining Italianità in the Long Nineteenth Century* (Cambridge University Press, 2022), 77–95.

[12] Rondy Torres, 'Tras las huellas armoniosas de una compañía lírica: La Rossi-D'Achiardi en Bogotá', *Revista del Instituto Carlos Vega* 26 (2012), 161–200.

bordering the Andes, roughly 4,500 kilometres from Guayaquil in Ecuador to Valparaiso in Chile, or the equivalent of driving from Lisbon to Moscow in a straight line.

As former Incan domains as well as former holdings of the Viceroyalty of Peru, these countries shared a long cultural, administrative and economic history. By the early 1800s, there were also enormous political, economic and social changes in the Andes. The Wars of Independence, fought during the 1810s and 1820s, fixed the borderlines of those new nations, and their early Republican histories. Lima, which had been the administrative and cultural centre during colonial times, lost ground during the 1830s to the new regional capitals (Quito, Sucre and Santiago) as well as to emerging ports, like Valparaiso and Guayaquil. The mythical allure of Peru, however, was still enormous, with stories about its wealth, and that of Potosi in Bolivia, freely circulating the globe. By the 1830s Valparaiso, on the coast of Chile, was the largest port on the South American Pacific coast, with a large population of immigrants from European nations.[13] Thus, performing artists slowly realized that, in terms of opera, there was enough interest in the region to make the trip worthwhile.

In comparison with research on the Caribbean and the Atlantic Coast of South America (Brazil and Argentina), there has been very little research on opera in the Andes. Particularly so for the period discussed here, the 1840s and 1850s.[14] But operatic reception in the Andes in the 1840s complicates the general assumptions about 'global opera' during the nineteenth century. By 1840, the foundations for the transatlantic operatic trade had been already established in other parts of the Americas, more accessible from Europe, like the southern Atlantic Coast (Rio de Janeiro, Buenos Aires) or the Caribbean and Circum-Caribbean region (Havana, New Orleans, Mexico City), as well as in the East Coast of the United States. But the Andes were widely seen as one of those 'last frontiers' for the establishment of operatic taste. The development of steam travel, as we will see, was essential to that process, since a stable connection

---

[13] In terms of Valparaiso as an economic port for the region, see the comments of Jorge León, *Evolución del comercio exterior y del transporte marítimo de Costa Rica 1821–1900* (Editorial Universidad de Costa Rica, 1997), 55–65. One of the best papers on commercial organizations in Valparaiso in this period, with more detailed information, is Eduardo Cavieres, 'Estructura y funcionamiento de las sociedades comerciales de Valparaiso durante el siglo XIX (1820–1880)', *Cuadernos de Historia* 4 (1984), 61–86.

[14] In terms of new perspectives on Italian opera and Italian opera reception in the Atlantic Coast of South America (Brazil, Uruguay and Argentina), but with a focus on the final decades of the nineteenth century, see Anibal Cetrangolo, *Ópera, barcos y banderas: El melodrama y la migración argentina* (Editorial Biblioteca Nueva, 2015); as well as the dossier edited by Vera Wolkowicz for the Revista Argentina de Musicología (2020, Volume 1), which includes chapters on the subject by Wolkowicz, Paoletti, and Walton.

between seaports became a fundamental element in developing a stable network for performing practices like opera.[15] I consider the 1840s as a foundational period of operatic practices in the Andes, when the genre changed from being one amongst others to a central feature of local cultural scenes. When seen retrospectively, the Pantanelli company set the foundations for a permanent operatic scene not only in Lima, but more generally in the Andean region.

For Italians in search of new lands to conquer for their operatic empire, the arrival of the Pantanelli company in the Andean region was a sign that 'our Italian opera is most certainly on the expansion', as the Milanese newspaper *Il Pirata* put it in 1844.[16] As a not-yet-unified country, Italy could not compete with the growing imperial expansion of European nations. Opera in turn often served as a mediated or indirect form of imperial project, what historians nowadays call an 'informal empire': based not on political or military domination, but on economic and cultural domination of networks, goods and ideas.[17] As Lucy Riall has argued, Italians in places like mid-nineteenth-century Lima 'thought and behaved colonially', because of their use of routes and networks, and their consciousness of the power and hierarchies of human mobility.[18]

But the empire of opera, like many other European imperial projects at the time, was only successful after a 'war' for domination; after battling and conquering several other forms of entertainment, amongst which it was only one more during the 1840s: Italian opera competed against the Spanish *tonadilla* tradition, musical comedies, dramatic companies, popular music and dance, as well as bullfighting. Opera, and opera singers, were not always welcomed with open hands, and the development of networks, businesses, audiences and a market for opera was a contested and difficult job, sometimes read as a form of cultural imposition. However, that was not necessarily so: we have to abandon the idea that operatic reception was a passive exercise. The agency of singers was central, overcoming disease and danger, moving to the other side of the world, overcoming the local resistance to opera. But the agency of audiences and brokers was also essential, in many different ways that, I hope, I will show through this Element.

In the following sections, I will explore these different issues, based on a decade of archival research in Ecuador, Chile, Peru and Bolivia, as well as

---

[15] Michael Walter, *Oper: Geschichte einer Institution* (J. B. Metzler, 2016), 120.

[16] *Il Pirata*, Milan, 4 January 1844.

[17] Jessie Reeder, *The Forms of Informal Empire: Britain, Latin America, and Nineteenth-Century Literature* (Johns Hopkins University Press, 2020).

[18] Lucy Riall, 'Un "Imperial Meridian" in Peru: Appeal, commercio e scienze dell'imperialismo informale italiano, 1848–1890'. Paper presented in the X Cantieri di Storia Sissco, Modena, 18–20 September 2019. www.sissco.it/wp-content/uploads/2019/07/Riall-Imperial-Meridian.pdf (Revised March 2022).

in Italy: how opera became relevant to new audiences, how it was canonized beyond European borders, how networks were developed, how theatres adapted to new business models and how technologies, politics and economics affected the availability of opera singers. I hope that this Element conveys something of the careful groundwork needed to lay the foundation of a new operatic scene. What I consider essential when thinking about opera 'abroad' in the mid-nineteenth century is that we cannot take the reception and expansion of Italian opera during this period for granted: it certainly didn't feel so to those working, listening or performing it beyond European shores in the 1840s. Each new city, each new work, each new way of dealing with the business of operatic performance, could (and often did) lead to failure. Looking at the Andes in the 1840s, it is my hope to show the very human actions that made opera possible in nineteenth-century Latin America.

1 Music and Theatre in the Andes Around 1840

Unlike Europe and other parts of the Americas, which already had expectations for Italian opera, in the Andes kick-starting an Italian opera scene was no easy task. Italian opera, during the 1840s and 1850s, was a hugely disruptive cultural force in the Andean region, even beyond urban centres. During the 1840s, as one contemporary writer put it, 'opera became a necessity' for the definition of contemporary, modern culture.[19] But the process by which it became a necessity was an arduous one. But to understand that disruption, we have to look at the context into which it arrived. Italian opera had to compete directly with entrenched local customs that were tied to a Spanish colonial past. Its success was determined by the kind of experiences in music theatre people had, what audiences might have expected of theatrical evenings, and the infrastructure that sustained such practices, which Italian opera used, learned from and irreversibly transformed in the span of a decade.

The idea that opera was disruptive, however, might not be entirely obvious when reading contemporary sources. Newspapers are the most important source for research on the study of nineteenth-century opera in Latin America. But one can be easily misled by those newspapers. Looking at early reviews in the Andes, it could seem as if Italian opera arrived into a vacuum, a blank theatrical slate in which it was instantly recognized as the only performing medium worthy of praise and respect. As one newspaper put it in 1840, just after the arrival of the Pantanelli company: 'opera is the most beautiful of ornaments for a capital city ... the most admired of arts, making us proud of the human spirit and its ingenuity'.[20] After the first operatic performance in 1842 in Guayaquil,

---

[19] *El Comercio*, Lima, 25 April 1848.   [20] *El Amigo del Pueblo*, Lima, 4 August 1840.

Ecuador, the local newspaper stated that 'Opera, as a goddess, chooses a simple building, perhaps safe and decent, and with a touch of its wand transforms it into a temple'.[21] When the Pantanellis arrived in Chile, in 1844, celebrated writer and politician Domingo Faustino Sarmiento wrote that the groundbreaking experience of live Italian opera was that of 'civilization in its most refined degree'.[22]

Sarmiento's quote is symptomatic of this early period of operatic reception. By the end of the century, and with the background of large urban migrations from southern Europe, Italian opera would be perceived by Latin American intellectual elites as a genre for ill-educated migrants. But in the 1840s, for the elites and middle classes of urban Latin America, opera was still considered in terms of both education (as theatre was in colonial times) and Europeanization as a form of modernity. Indeed, this was a period of rapid Europeanization, in customs, ideas and fashions. Central Europe served as a model, a way of becoming modern while, at the same time, defining that modernity in direct contrast to Spain and the colonial past. Thus, in newspapers, Italian opera was often used as a way of highlighting the contrasts between local culture and the imagined and idealized possibilities of a more European Latin America. And to go back to Sarmiento: he wrote that quote while serving as the preeminent opera critic in Chile, when the Pantanelli company arrived in 1844. At that same time, he was also finishing his most influential book, *Facundo: Civilization and Barbarism*. In that book, Sarmiento used the notions of civilization and barbarism as poles to identify trends that defined, according to him, contemporary Latin American culture. Barbarism was the Indigenous, the rural, the Spanish, the colonial; civilization was the modern, the urban, Europe, Italian opera.

But Italian opera, even if heralded as the vanguard of civilization in the form of European culture, arrived in a theatrical context still shaped by colonial structures, institutions, buildings and forms of entertainment. For example, it had to be performed in colonial theatres. There were many theatres in the late-colonial Andean region, perhaps only the one in Lima could have been called a proper theatre. Most theatrical venues, traditionally known as *coliseos* or *corrales*, were temporary buildings, often without a roof, and certainly without orchestra pit. Lima's theatre, a model for others in the region, was built in 1766, during the government of Viceroy Manuel de Amat. Amat, grounded in the ideas of Enlightenment, certainly believed that theatre and music could serve not only to entertain but to civilize and create morally grounded citizens.[23]

---

[21] *Correo Semanal de Guayaquil*, Guayaquil, 25 September 1842.

[22] *El Progreso*, Santiago, 27 April 1844.

[23] Rolando Rojas, *Tiempos de carnaval, el Ascenso de los popular a la cultura nacional, Lima 1822–1922* (Instituto Francés de Estudios Andinos, 2005), 45.

With the expulsion of the Jesuits during Amat's period, and the enormous lack of literacy in the population, theatre and music were perceived as ways in which moral ideas could be communicated in an efficient way. According to Rolando Rojas, what was promoted was the learned stage: 'while other forms of representation were censored, like comedies and parodies of saints' lives ... theatre was considered the best way to communicate specific ideas and values, educate the people into moral and civic ideas'.[24] This way of thinking about the theatre as a public space had serious implications, as we will see, for later ways of appreciating Italian opera during the nineteenth century.

Amat believed that music and plays had to be preferred over other forms of entertainment, like street performances, and bull and cock fighting.[25] The theatre was perceived as a place for education, particularly for the illiterate masses. Its impact is statistically self-evident: at the top of its capacity, a theatre like the Coliseo in Lima, even by the 1830s, could fill 4 per cent of the adult population of the city. It was four times more than the reach of any of the local newspapers.[26] However, as a venue, it left much to be desired. In the opinion of Henry Wise, an English traveller in 1849, 'the immense rafters that uphold the flat roof are apt to keep a nervous person in the pit somewhat anxious and uneasy, anticipating a shock of the tremor. It is sufficiently commodious, but badly ventilated, dimly lighted, and without decorations'.[27] Wise also complained about the abundance of flies, as did the German traveller Johann Tschudi, who attended a play in 1838.[28] Locals didn't have a much better opinion of the venue: Manuel Atanasio Fuentes, in his *Sketches of Lima*, considered that, while it could hold up to 1,500 persons, in reality it was 'altogether unworthy of a civilised nation'.[29] Basil Hall, who visited the place in the 1820s, gives us a more detailed look at the place:

> [The Coliseo in Lima is] of a rather singular form; being a long oval, the stage occupying the greater part of one side, by which means the front boxes were brought close to the actors. The audience in the pit was composed exclusively

[24] Rolando Rojas, 'La república imaginada: representaciones culturales y discursos políticos en la independencia peruana (Lima, 1821–1822)', unpublished MA thesis, Universidad Mayor de San Marcos (2009), 58.

[25] Juan Carlos Estenssoro, 'La Plebe Ilustrada: El Pueblo en las Fronteras de la Razón', in Charles Walker (ed.), *Entre la retórica y la insurgencia: Las ideas y los movimientos sociales en los Andes, siglo XVIII* (Centro Bartolomé de las Casas, 1995), 55.

[26] Mónica Ricketts, 'El teatro en Lima y la construcción de la nación republicana (1820–1850)', unpublished BA thesis, Pontificia Universidad Católica de Lima (1996), 49.

[27] Henry August Wise, *Los Gringos, Or an Inside View of Mexico and California, with Wanderings in Peru, Chili and Polynesia* (R. Bentley, 1849), 395.

[28] Johann Jakob von Tschudi, *Peru: Reiseskizzen aus den Jahren 1838-1842* (Scheitlin und Zollifoker, 1846), 60.

[29] Manuel Atanasio Fuentes, *Lima: Or, Sketches of the Capital of Peru* (Trübner, 1866), 70.

of men, and that in the galleries of women ... the intermediate space was divided into several rows of private boxes. Between the acts, the Viceroy retires to the back seat of his box, which being taken as a signal that he may be considered as absent, every man in the pit draws forth his steel and flint, lights his cigar, and puffs away vigorously, in order to make the most of his time; for when the curtain rises, and the Viceroy again comes forward, there can no longer be any smoking, consistently with Spanish etiquette. ... The Viceroy's presence or absence, however, produces no change in the gallery aloft, where the goddesses keep up an unceasing fire during the whole evening.[30]

Inside that venue, and other less prominent theatres in Santiago, or Guayaquil, or La Paz, there had been, until the 1840s, very few opportunities to see Italian opera performed on a stage by professional Italian singers. There had been opera in the Andes for a long time: indeed, the earliest opera composed in Latin America is *La Púrpura de la Rosa*, premiered in 1701 with music by Tomás de Torrejón y Velasco. But, as far as we know, only in 1812 there was for the first time a season of Italian opera in Lima, sung in Italian and performed by Italian singers: Pietro Angelelli and Carolina Griffoni, who came from Europe and previously sung, apparently, in Buenos Aires and Montevideo.[31] They worked alongside successful actors and actresses, like Rosa Merino, and under the direction of the music director of Lima Cathedral, the Italian cellist Andrea Bolognesi, who most probably arranged for their visit and the repertoire, consisting of operas by Cimarosa and Paisiello.

The period between the arrival of Angelelli and Griffoni in 1812, through the performances of the Schieroni and Pizzoni company in the early 1830s, down to the arrival of the Pantanelli company in 1840, was one of enormous disruption to local musical practices. On the one hand, Italian opera created an economic disruption, making much more money than it was usual for local artists. Already in 1812, Pietro Angelelli, in a public letter defending himself of several accusations from the manager of the theatre, wrote that, while 'no one imagined here that Italian opera singers could arrive', and 'while we only worked on days in which no *comedias* were performed', opera made much more money in a month that would have been expected from any previous season.[32]

On the other hand, Italian opera reshaped tastes and practices. In Spain, the issue of Italian opera disrupting local practices had become thorny already in the late eighteenth century. Many tonadillas made fun of Italian teachers, 'Italian'

---

[30] Basil Hall, *Extracts from a Journal: Written on the Coasts of Chili, Peru, and Mexico, in the Years 1820, 1821 and 1822* (A. Constable, 1826), Volume 1, 108–9.

[31] Pedro Angelelli, *Habiendo llegado a nuestras manos [...]* (Imprenta de los Huérfanos, 1812). Original preserved in the Biblioteca Nacional del Perú, code 4000001577.

[32] Angelelli, *Habiendo llegado a nuestras manos.*

melismatic singing in the Neapolitan style, or Italian opera more directly.[33] At
the turn of the century, a protectionist move by Charles IV of Spain sentenced
that 'in no theatre in the realms of Spain can there be pieces performed in
a language that is not Spanish, or by actors and actresses that are nationals of
these realms'.[34] The Napoleonic wars debilitated the protectionist move but, at
least between 1800 and 1808, there was a direct prohibition for any musical
theatre that was not in Spanish, fostering the popularity of Spanish forms of
entertainment, the repertoires that would later set the foundations of the romantic zarzuela tradition.

On the other hand, Andean cities were influenced by practices and repertoires in the viceregal
capital of Lima; and Lima, in turn, by trends in Spain. There were two predom-
inant forms of musical theatre in Andean stages at this time, against which
Italian opera had to compete directly: *comedias* and *tonadillas*. Comedias were
plays in which certain parts were sung by performers, mostly *commedia del-
l'arte* in style, but also some with religious topics (*comedias de santos*).
Religious comedies, frequently not very saintly and often censored by the
Catholic church, were extremely popular. In Lima, for example, the most
popular piece in the 1820s and well into the 1830s was a comedy with songs,
El diablo predicador (The Preaching Devil), which was often proscribed by the
Church and attacked by the press.[35] A handful of songs coming from some of
these plays can be found today in the Biblioteca Nacional del Perú, with
educational texts set to the kind of music also found in the tradition of the
villancico, sacred music in vernacular language.[36]

On the other hand, tonadillas were a form of short musical play, lasting from
10 to 20 minutes, extremely popular in Spain and its colonies during the second
half of the eighteenth century and, in certain regions like Venezuela, well into
the 1840s.[37] Tonadillas were often performed in between acts from larger
dramas, or at the beginning or the end of an evening. There was an important
reason for the popularity of tonadillas: like Italian *intermezzi*, they were often

---

[33] Elisabeth Le Guin, *The Tonadilla in Performance: Lyric Comedy in Enlightenment Spain*
(University of California Press, 2013), 76, 102.

[34] For the original document, see José Garriga, *Continuación y suplemento del Prontuario de don
Severo Aguirre* (Librería de don Valentín Francés, 1802), 323–7.

[35] Ricketts, 'El teatro en Lima', 34. The piece also parodied an influential piece of dramatic theatre,
also titled *El diablo predicador*, written by Luis Belmonte Bermúdez, who lived in Mexico and
Peru in the seventeenth century.

[36] The Biblioteca Nacional del Perú has a large collection of music manuscripts from the nineteenth
century that has only been partially catalogued. I was able to consult the music thanks to the help
of Laura Martínez, then head of collections in the National Library, but it is not accessible for the
general public.

[37] Montserrat Capelán, 'La tonadilla escénica en Venezuela o el proceso de criollización de un
género hispano', *Anuario Musical* 72 (2017), 137–52.

composed or adapted to depict contemporary social life, with an immediacy of verbal and musical language, and a defining popular character; thus, they could be easily reused to fit new audiences, or new local or global topics and debates.[38] That was indeed the case in the Andes, where local tonadillas even allowed for patriotic discourses, using the framework of an eminently Spanish form of musical theatre to convey the new 'national' spirit of independence.[39]

Already in 1812, *El Investigador*, a prominent newspaper in that last decade of colonial rule in Peru, had to publish a series of instructions on how listening to opera differed from attending performances of tonadillas and comedias:

> Three things are needed to appreciate it, in my opinion: 1. To be extremely attentive . . ., in silence; a profound silence has to reign in the temple of Apollo; 2. To understand music a little [*mediano oído y gusto músico*], which is only possible by getting rid of the old tonadillas, guaraguas and old musics, and studying the modern [*actuales*] operas, not neglecting the instrumental parts; 3. To learn beforehand what is going to be sung, which can be done by asking those with knowledge . . . I do not understand a word of Italian, but after listening twice to an aria I can understand more or less what it is about.[40]

The idea that Italian opera needed something different from audiences, or that it was ontologically different from other forms of music theatre, comes forward with increasing strength during the 1820s and 1830s, a period in which there were very few operatic performances in the region. There were some lonely travelling Italian singers: Vincenzo Zapucci, for example, travelled in 1823 from Havana to Buenos Aires, later performing in Lima with Teresa Schieroni and Domingo Pizzoni.[41] He traversed the region during the 1820s and 1830s, going as far as Guayaquil with his wife Teresa Nattini.[42] In Chile, Isidora Zegers, a Spanish soprano who had studied with Frédéric Massimino in Paris, popularized the works of Rossini during the 1820s and 1830s, but mostly from the comfort of her home, rather than on the stage. Sometimes, local actors and actresses performed music, in particular arias by Rossini, in between acts or for their benefits.[43]

The other way in which people listened to opera during the 1820s and 1830s was in the form of vocal scores and instrumental arrangements, performed at home or by military bands. Vincenzo Massoni, who lived in Chile between 1826 and 1830, and later moved to Peru following Pizzoni and Schieroni, formed one

---

[38] Le Guin, *The Tonadilla in Performance*, 143.

[39] José Manuel Izquierdo, '*El Militar Retirado de Pedro Ximénez Abrill* (Arequipa, 1784 – Sucre, 1856): Una tonadilla inedita en el Perú independiente', *Diagonal: An Ibero-American Music Review* 1/2 (2016).

[40] *El Investigador*, Lima, 12 July 1813.   [41] *El Mercurio Peruano*, Lima, 15 June 1832.

[42] Archivo Público del Guayas, Causas Criminales 1827/4.

[43] *El Mercurio*, Valparaiso, 12 August 1828.

of the first dedicated music stores in the region, in Valparaiso, where he sold 'music for all instruments, voice and piano, and all the operas by Rossini, as well as other composers'.[44] In Chile, music scores and instruments had been declared tax-free in 1820, Valparaiso being the free port of entry.[45] One of the best examples of the way such scores circulated and were performed is the album belonging to Jesús Urriola, probably compiled in 1836 and now preserved in the *Teatro Municipal*, the main opera house in Santiago, Chile. The album includes more than a dozen pieces by Rossini, arranged for four-hands, in the form of piano fantasies, or as translated songs in Spanish.[46]

But even if only through scores, isolated performances and amateur singers, Italian opera was already making an impact, its disruption becoming much more concrete. In particular, Italian opera presented a direct form of competition to tonadillas. In 1831, according to an inventory of the Coliseo in Lima which was drafted by the members of the orchestra, the archive included no less than 13 operas, 28 'operettas' (a word used at the time for vaudevilles and early zarzuelas) and 36 boxes of tonadillas, each one with 10 to 20 pieces each: around 500 tonadillas in total, more or less.[47] By the mid-1830s, the same musicians considered that 'all of these scores are useless nowadays', even if they comprised 'most of what the archive possesses' and thus could not even be sold off.[48]

But tonadillas were still being performed in 1840. Even on August 1840, when the Pantanelli company arrived, one could find in Lima an evening like this, as fitting for the 1820s as it had been for the 1790s, in its structure as well as in the genres being performed: 'The Young Husband and the Old Woman, a comedy in three acts, followed by the well-known *tonadilla Los Indios*, and the saynete [a comic scene] *Las Besuqueras*.'[49] But these were the very last tonadillas, and the very last evenings with such formats. For Felipe Pardo y Aliaga, writing in 1840, the Pantanelli company – and Italian opera more generally – was not a problem on itself, but rather because of the ways in which local audiences were appreciating Italian opera as performed by them. If Italian opera represented a certain kind of modernity, civilization and progress, it was a kind that directly confronted Andean identity and cultural practices as defined by the Spanish colonial past. But the Pantanelli company marked a point of no return: it consolidated the acceptance of Italian opera as a repertoire, and it kick-started a regular series of

[44] *El Mercurio de Valparaíso*, Valparaiso, 2 April 1828.
[45] *Gazeta Extraordinaria Ministerial*, Santiago, 9 October 1820.
[46] José Manuel Izquierdo, 'Rossini's Reception in Latin America: Scarcity and Imagination in Two Early Chilean Sources', in Ilaria Narici, Emilio Sala, Emanuele Senici and Benjamin Walton (eds.), *Gioachino Rossini 1868–2018* (Pesaro: Fondazione Rossini, 2018), 413–36.
[47] Pablo Macera, *Teatro Peruano, siglo XIX* (Universidad Nacional Mayor de San Marcos, 1991).
[48] Macera, *Teatro Peruano*, 2.   [49] *El Comercio*, Lima, 29 August 1840.

operatic performances that would continue until the early twentieth century. Quoting Felipe Pardo y Aliaga:

> [Italian opera arrived] and suddenly everyone considered that an aria from *Romeo* is a thousand times more valuable than all the songs from la Chepa Manteca [a popular singer at the time]; or that the trial of Crispo in *Fausta* easily surpasses the tonadilla of *El Correjidor* (Do you even remember it? . . .). Well, summing up, now everyone believes that Italian opera is better than any of our creole, local ones.[50]

2 The Frameworks for Italian Opera

Italian opera was not only a modern form of art that competed against local forms of cultural practice. It irrupted in 1840 as a definitive sign of progress, enabled by new technologies like steamships, overcoming the issues of mobility that had affected previous generations of performing artists. Italian opera, like steamers, was often read at this time as a symbol of the transformations in the world, the rapid rise of industrial modernity that was now also reaching beyond the Atlantic coasts. Like steamers, it connected the Andes to the rest of the world. And, also like steamers, its internal workings felt like magic: the quality of the voices, the impact of the drama, the scenery that transported the audience to other parts of the globe, with an immediacy that had been, until then, unknown. As a reviewer of the first operatic performances in Guayaquil put it, in 1842: 'The goddess of Opera works her magic, and we can feel, for a night, as if we were in Lima, or Janeiro, or Paris, London, Madrid or Milan, three thousand leagues from here, when we have not left Guayaquil. Isn't that wonderful? The Empire of Opera.'[51] Another writer, in Santiago de Chile in 1851, put it in even more expressive terms:

> Nowadays, miracles have fallen out of fashion, . . . and pacts with the devil are discredited, because science can now produce all of those things that evil spirits could not. We can now climb to the skies in a piece of cloth, or go around the world in a few days with the power of a boiler . . . or destroy a mountain with black powder . . . But we need wonders, as we need air, and men have invented a way to supply that wonder . . . opera is the highest expression of that new kind of magic that overwhelms the senses. Men pay nowadays for a vague sound, carried by the wind, more than kings of old had in gold.[52]

There were structural and technological reasons that explain why opera became both successful and stable in the 1840s in the Andes, including political and

---

[50] Felipe Pardo y Aliaga, *Poesías y escritos en prosa de don Felipe Pardo* (A. Chaix et cie, 1869), 347.

[51] *Correo Semanal de Guayaquil*, Guayaquil, 25 September 1842.

[52] *El Progreso*, Santiago, 20 August 1851.

economic stability, technological innovations and important social changes. During colonial times, connections between Peru and the rest of the world were slow and inefficient, shaped by the desire of Spanish control over its resources, both human and material. In the early nineteenth century, human and material movements were also crippled by the costs of the Wars of Independence (1808–26). The wars not only devastated local economies and the social landscape, but also created new frontiers and disentangled old connections. On top of that, the Andean region, being both mountainous and dry, was difficult to traverse, with few modern roads and, by the 1820s, a fully disrupted naval commerce.

In 1838, the entrepreneur William Wheelwright founded the Pacific Steam Navigation Company, to connect the ports of Guayaquil, Callao/Lima and Valparaiso through a network of steamers, and prepare the region for a direct route to Liverpool. The steamers *Peru* and *Chile* departed England in July 1840, crossing the Straits of Magellan and arriving in the Andes in October that same year. Other ships, like the *Ecuador*, the *Nueva Granada* and the *Bolivia*, reinforced the fleet between 1846 and 1850, reinforcing the social, economic and administrative connections between the countries on the American South Pacific.[53]

It is difficult today to measure the impact of these steamers in the economic, cultural and social life of the Andean region. The trip from Lima to Valparaiso, which previously could have taken a month in bad weather, could now be traversed in a week. Newspapers were quick to point out that, instead of months, steamers now travelled from Plymouth to Chile in less than sixty days, changing on the ports of Panama. But steamers even managed to cross Cape Horn, one of the most dangerous routes in the world, during the winter.[54] The first steamers were received in Valparaiso with artillery salutes, military bands and hundreds of boats filled with people wanting to see the wondrous machines. With the power of 100 horses, capacity for 150 people and 300 tonnes of commodities, they represented the arrival of the modern era to nations that only twenty years before had been under the rule of Spanish colonial law.

The connection between their arrival, and that of the Pantanelli company, was not lost to contemporary writers. Heinrich Witt, a businessman in Lima, wrote in his memoirs about both events as if they were one: '[That year] the steamers of the Pacific Steam Navigation Comp[an]y. commenced plying along the Coast; the two first were the "Peru" and "Chile." Also, about that time, a company of lyric performers appeared on the Lima Stage; the two Prima Donnas were Pantanelli and Rossi, who were received here with extraordinary

---

[53] Ian Collard, *Pacific Steam Navigation Company: Fleet List & History* (Amberley, 2014).
[54] *El Mercurio de Valparaíso*, Valparaiso, 3 October 1840.

applause'.[55] Felipe Pardo y Aliaga, a member of the aristocratic Limenian elite, published in 1840 one of his most famous novels: *Un viaje*, in which Goyito, the protagonist, decides to go to Chile for the first time, on a trip that his entire family still considers a crazy and dangerous endeavour. That same year, Pardo wrote his essay titled 'Opera and Nationalism', in which he criticizes the conservatives in Lima who behaved 'like enemies of opera' until they listened, as if transfigured, to the opera company for the first time.[56] In both works, the arrival of modernity (steamers and Italian opera) is felt as a danger to family, customs and tradition.

Michael Walter, in his recent account of opera as a global institution, agrees that South America, like Asia or Australia, opened to Italian opera companies at the time it did, because of the 'better and faster maritime transport' developed during the first half of the nineteenth century.[57] But the 1840s were still, at least for the Andean region, a transitional period. The Pantanellis, and their company, had to traverse the Caribbean by ship, from Havana in Cuba to Chagres, Panama (then part of Colombia), crossing the isthmus on horseback, and then travelling more than a month in a brig to arrive in Lima, with long and irregular stops in all the tropical ports in between. But Lima was the best destination, not only because it was the historic capital of the region. The only two major cities in the South American Pacific coast before Lima, Bogotá and Quito, the capitals of Colombia and Ecuador, respectively, were in the middle of the Andean plateau, and between one and two months were often needed to reach them on horseback or boat from the coast. This simple fact seriously impeded the development of an operatic scene in both cities until much later, in the 1870s, when steamers and trains allowed for shorter travelling times into the mountains.

By the end of the 1840s, maritime steam travel had become essential not only for the movement of goods (and singers) across the Andean region; it also became essential to convince new singers to come to the Andean region directly from Italy to perform for one or two years in Peru and Chile. In 1849, one reviewer in Lima commented on the fact that the quality of the singers could be gathered beforehand simply by knowing if they had travelled 'in a schooner, through Cape Horn' or by steamer, across Panama.[58] As an example, the contract for prima donna Lucrezia Micciarelli, signed in Milan in 1847, to perform in Peru and Chile for two seasons from 1848 to 1850, stated that the travel by sea had to be in 'the best and most comfortable' medium possible, and paid by the impresario.[59] She, and the rest of the company hired by Antonio

---

[55] Heinrich Witt, *The Diary of Heinrich Witt* (Brill, 2016), 296.
[56] Pardo y Aliaga, *Poesías y escritos*, 347.   [57] Walter, *Oper: Geschichte einer Institution*, 52.
[58] *El Comercio*, Lima, 2 January 1849.
[59] Archivo Histórico Republicano, AAM, ROJ428, no. 10.

Neumane, departed Milan after Christmas 1847, arriving by steamer in Lima in the early days of March, 'only' two months later.[60]

More importantly, steamers made it possible for opera to function as a network. To turn any opera company profitable, it was necessary to establish certain networks of cities, to offer the repertoire and the voices to different audiences during a period of time that covered the cost and danger of travelling from Europe. In the Andes, impresarios began to consider the Andean region as a cultural 'scene', with Lima and Valparaiso/Santiago as the focal points. As one newspaper editor put it in 1844, 'it would be impossible to sustain an opera company with just the audience in Lima, there are just not enough people'.[61] This network, based on steamers and the transit of people and commodities, was further reinforced by the development of new theatres that connected operatic performances across the region. The steamers traversed a fixed route alongside the coast, connecting a number of ports, most of which were visited by Italian opera singers for the first time during this decade. While the route was centred around Valparaiso in Chile and Callao in Peru (the port of Lima), other towns grew in numbers alongside the steaming routes. From north to south, the main ports were Guayaquil, Paita, Lambayeque, Trujillo, Callao, Mollendo (the port of Arequipa), Arica (also connecting Tacna), Iquique, Cobija (the old port of Bolivia), Copiapo, Coquimbo, Valparaiso and, at the end of the route, Talcahuano, the port of Concepción.

The problem is that, while steamers connected Andean cities, almost none of them had a proper theatre. If they had one, it had been built in colonial times, often without a roof, and most certainly without an orchestra pit. But now that steamers increased the chances of being visited by an opera company, a sure sign of modernity which most cities were eager to welcome, many of those theatres were remodelled, and many others built from scratch. A theatre was often the first major public building commissioned during Republican times: as one writer in La Paz, Bolivia, put it, 'other public works are not as urgent, and they should wait until the theatre is finished'.[62] Theatres were now considered central features of a modern city in the image of grand European capitals, but it was also still believed that the central role of those theatres was to educate a mostly illiterate population, serving as a mirror in which people could contemplate themselves and their attitudes.[63]

As a combination of these two ideals, theatres were often described at the time as another form of technology: barometers or thermometers, modern scientific tools used 'by travellers to know the degree of civilization of a city',

---

[60] *El Comercio*, Lima, 10 March 1848.   [61] *El Comercio*, Lima, 17 February 1844.
[62] *La Época*, La Paz, 16 May 1845.   [63] *El Araucano*, Santiago, 13 June 1835.

as one promoter of a new theatre in Quito, Ecuador, put it.[64] In this, perhaps, one can see a common trend with provincial town in Europe, and even in Italy, at the time, where theatres were perceived in similar ways. It was necessary to have one.[65] In South America, the main tool to measure that thermometer were European travellers' accounts, which often include a description of the local theatre of each of the cities they visit. Descriptions most often describe both the building and the behaviour of the people inside it. Theatres work as a marker, a standardized product that could be easily compared from place to place, connecting European readers with a common framework that also includes theatres back home. While the books were printed in French, German or English, they were sometimes translated into Spanish for the consumption of readers in Latin America, including as *foulletins* inside newspapers, and thus also reaching a local audience.

Regulations are another marker of these ideals. For example, the 1849 regulation for the theatres of Lima specifies that no 'uncivilised' plays should be performed, and that the aim of the theatre is to give people a sense of virtue, asking for a censoring body to control the content of the plays and operas being performed.[66] When Domingo Arteaga and architect Vicente Caballero built a new theatre in Santiago, in 1820, the drape contained the following words by Chilean poet Bernardo Vera y Pintado: 'Here is the mirror of virtue and vice; see yourself in it, and pronounce your judgement.'[67] Another, even more public example of this trend was the words Ecuadorian poet José Joaquín Olmedo wrote for two of these venues. First, for the theatre in Lima: 'I support virtue, and bring down vice; and I guide the people, through entertainment, into a healthy morale.' The other one appeared not on the drape, but on the façade of the new theatre in Guayaquil, inaugurated in 1857, with the words being clearly visible in many photographs of the period: 'A mirror of our manners is the theatre: those who refuse to come fear the reflection; those who criticise it, only condemn themselves.'[68]

The first new theatre in the Andean region built with Italian opera in mind was the *Teatro Victoria*, in front of the square of that same name in Valparaiso, Chile. It was inaugurated by the Pantanelli company with a performance of Bellini's *Capuleti* in 1844. The theatre was the idea of Pietro Alessandri, an

---

[64] *Crónica del Teatro*, Quito, 13 September 1877.

[65] Carlotta Sorba, *Politics and Sentiments in Risorgimento Italy: 'Melodrama and the Nation'* (Palgrave Macmillan, 2021). See, in particular, Chapter 2 and the ways new entertainment spaces in large capitals like London and Paris were modelled back to other smaller cities across Europe.

[66] *Reglamento para los teatros públicos del Perú* (Imprenta de E. Aranda, 1849), 11.

[67] Miguel Luis Amunátegui, *Las primeras representaciones dramáticas en Chile* (Imprenta Nacional, 1888), 52.

[68] Emilio Carilla, 'Revisión de Olmedo', *Thesaurus* 19/1 (1964), 135.

Italian puppeteer-turned-businessman in Chile. Clorinda Corradi, in a private letter to the German painter Moritz Rugendas, considered it 'one of the best in the Americas'.[69] Her husband, Raffaele Pantanelli, also described it as 'magnificent' in a letter to his friend Gaetano Fiori.[70] It was designed to feel European. Even before performances started, through its architecture and decoration, it created an experience for the audience: to feel as if being transported to Europe. Its French architect, Pierre Claveaux, based his work on imported European drawings.[71] French traveller Jacques Arago echoed those intentions when he described the theatre as 'large, well decorated, comfortable and with a certain luxury. [... It] could rival the finest [*des plus beaux*] of Europe [... making us] forget that four thousand leagues separate Valparaíso from Paris'.[72]

The Teatro Municipal in La Paz, Bolivia, which still survives, was finished a year later, in 1845. Its shape was clearly inspired by Italian, rather than Spanish, colonial models, even if it was built by a local architect.[73] Hugh Bonelli, visiting the city in the late 1840s, considered it 'a respectable and commodious building, possessing four tiers of boxes, which, as far as can be discerned by the feeble aid of mere tallow candles, appear to be very decently decorated'.[74] An opera company was not available for the inauguration in 1845 (the first opera performances were in 1847), but an Italian bandmaster, Benedetto Vincenti, was hired in Valparaiso by the Bolivian government for the occasion.[75] The inauguration included instrumental arrangements of opera selections by Donizetti and Auber, as well as a new patriotic song by Vincenti that would later become the National Anthem of Bolivia.[76]

Some of these new theatres were comparatively[?] small. The mining boom in Copiapo, in the north of Chile, led to the construction of a theatre there in 1848, a roofless building that worked well in that arid climate.[77] The Pantanellis inaugurated it, during their return trip from Lima to Valparaiso in

[69] Gertrud Richert, 'La correspondencia del pintor alemán Juan Mauricio Rugendas', *Boletín de la Academia Chilena de la Historia* 19/1 (1952), 150.

[70] *Teatri, arti e letteratura*, Bologna, 29 August 1844.

[71] José Manuel Izquierdo, 'The Invention of an Opera House: The 1844 Teatro Victoria in Valparaiso, Chile', *Cambridge Opera Journal* 32/2 (2021), 129–53.

[72] Jacques Arago, *Deux Océans* (Kiessling, Schnée et Cie., 1954), 184.

[73] María Eugenia Soux, 'La música en la ciudad de La Paz, 1845–1885', unpublished BA thesis, Universidad Mayor de San Andrés (1992), 29.

[74] Hugh de Bonelli, *Travels in Bolivia: With a Tour Across the Pampas to Buenos Ayres* (Hurst and Blackett, 1854), 206.

[75] Archivo Nacional de Chile, Notarios de Valparaíso, Victorio Martínez, V70: 108.

[76] *La Época*, La Paz, 17 November 1845. With respect to Italian composers and their relationships to Latin American national anthems, see Federico Gon, 'Gli "eroi dei due mondi": Rossini, Donizetti, Verdi e gli inni nazionali sudamericani', in Roberto Iliano (ed.), *VIVA V.E.R.D.I.: Music from Risorgimento to the Unification of Italy* (Brepols, 2013), 1–18.

[77] Eugenio Pereira Salas, *Historia de la Música en Chile 1850–1900* (Editorial Universitaria, 1950), 16.

1849.[78] A similar one was built in Lambayeque, in the northern coast of Peru, with a single row of boxes and capacity for less than 900 people. It was inaugurated by an opera company led by Paolo Ferretti, a member of the Pantanelli company since 1842, and his wife the soprano María España.[79] During the 1850s secondary smaller theatres began to compete with the main venues in larger cities, as in Santiago, Valparaiso and Lima. This increased the number of companies that could perform in the city at the same time. The first of this, the *Variedades*, was built in Lima by Alexander Tessiérer and Charles Zuderell, French impresarios, with a focus on dramatic performances and small concerts. Its capacity of 900 was half that of the *Teatro Principal*, the old colonial theatre, but as a venue it was much more modern and comfortable, attracting a good-sized audience.[80]

What this technological network of steamers and theatres produced was not only a framework for opera seasons to become viable and profitable, but also a much more interconnected Andean theatrical and performing arts scene. Audiences began to perceive their operatic scene in terms of an Andean region, rather than only as a local urban phenomenon. The press was central in this process, since newspapers circulated widely and effectively, thanks to regular steamers. In 1842, a letter was printed in Valparaiso, praising the performances of Teresa Rossi and Clorinda Corradi in Lima and urging some impresario to bring them to Chile. That same letter was later reprinted in Guayaquil, with a month of difference.[81] Teresa Rossi never sang in Bolivia, but a *foulletin* published in Lima about a poet who becomes deliriant while listening to her was later reprinted in La Paz, giving readers a narrative glimpse of the famous star.[82] Of course, often Valparaiso and Santiago competed about which city had the best audience or performers.[83] When Clorinda Corradi was criticized in Valparaiso in 1847 for her performance as Rosina in *Barbiere*, the critic stated that his opinion was shared 'from the Rímac to the Bio-Bio [the rivers in Lima on the north and Concepción in the south], by audiences in Lima, Valparaiso and Santiago'.[84] The Andean operatic scene was, by then, fully shaped in the imaginations of its audience.

---

[78] *El Comercio*, Lima, 2 January 1849. Andrea Rodríguez Silva, 'Los orígenes del Teatro en Copiapó', unpublished MA thesis, Universidad de Chile (2003), 75.

[79] Jorge Izquierdo Castañeda, 'El desaparecido teatro de Lambayeque', *Semanario Clarín Chiclayo*, 5 November 2017. http://semanarioclarin-chiclayo.blogspot.com/2017/11/el-desaparecido-treatro-de-lambayeque.html (Revised 16 March 2022).

[80] David Carlos Rengifo, 'Le théâtre historique et la construction de la nation: essor, crise et résurgence: Lima 1848–1924', unpublished PhD thesis, Université Rennes 2 (2018), 81.

[81] *El Mercurio de Valparaíso*, Valparaiso, 25 December 1841; *Correo Semanal de Guayaquil*, Guayaquil, 6 February 1842.

[82] *La Época*, La Paz, 9 August 1848.

[83] *El Mercurio de Valparaíso*, Valparaiso, 15 April 1850.

[84] *El Mercurio de Valparaíso*, Valparaiso, 16 February 1847.

3 A Disruptive Form of Business

Opera is a form of business and, in the words of Philippe Agid and Jean-Claude Tarondeau, 'an opera company [has], time and time again, proved to be the most effective vehicle for delivering consistent and high performance quality'.[85] In previous sections, I have defined the main group of artists who performed opera in the Andean region as the Pantanelli company. But there is much to say about how exactly the business of opera was carried out in the Andes, and how did opera companies work at the time. This is not just a technical issue: whether opera was considered as a 'civilizing' force or not, it took a lot of work to make Italian opera happen in Latin America. And this was by no means a passive process, or one immediately accepted by locals. In fact, it was a complicated and nuanced operation carried out by different people, at different times and places.

There were two business models in operation during the 1840s that brought opera to the Andean region: the first one was to organize a small opera company from singers already working in Havana (or later, mainly from the 1860s on, in Buenos Aires). The main 'source' for those companies were singers whose contracts expired and either did not return or did not want to return to Europe. The second model required travel to Italy (or at the very least an agent in Italy) in order to hire a number of singers through local contacts and newspaper advertisements. In both cases, singers were generally hired to perform in the Andean region for two years. During the 1840s, one can trace six moments in which opera companies were formed with, at least in part, new artists from Europe. It was not uncommon, however, for singers from these companies to take on new projects, or to be joined by new independent artists who had been travelling as teachers, or as partners of other migrants. The companies of the 1840s were:

1. The 1840 Pantanelli company (Havana to Lima): Raffaele Pantanelli (conductor, impresario), Gaetano Guadaroli (concertino), Antonio Meucci (decorations), Teresa Rossi (soprano, prima donna), Clorinda Corradi-Pantanelli (contralto, seconda donna), Andres Sissa (Milanese tenor, who had been performing in Mexico for several years), José Marti (a Cuban tenor), Nestor Corradi (brother of Clorinda), Maria España (a local soprano), Vincenzo Zapucci (the old tenor who convinced them to travel to Peru).

2. The 1842 Bazzani/Neumane Company (Havana/Lima to Guayaquil): Antonio Neumane (conductor, impresario), Idalide Turri (soprano, Neumane's wife), Teresa Rossi (soprano), Alessandro Zambaiti (tenor, also brought from Lima),

---

[85] Philippe Agid and Jean-Claude Tarondeau, *The Management of Opera: An International Comparative Study* (Palgrave Macmillan, 2010), x.

Paolo Ferretti (baritone), Luigi Grandi (basso), Gastaldi (basso), Rizzoli (tenor, leader of the choir), Luigi Bazzani (costume designer).

3. The 1844 Pantanelli company (Lima to Valparaiso): Raffaele Pantanelli (impresario, conductor), Teresa Rossi (soprano, prima donna), Clorinda Corradi-Pantanelli (contralto), Paolo Ferretti (basso), Nestor Corradi (tenor), Luigi Grandi (basso), Alessandro Zambaiti (tenor), José Martí (basso), María España (soprano), Raffaele Giorgi (decorations), Luigi Bazzani (costume designer).

4. The 1846 Bazzani Company (Milan to Valparaiso): Luigi Bazzani (costume designer turned impresario), Gaetano Bastoggi (basso assoluto), Teresa Pusterla (soprano, prima donna and Bastoggi's wife), Gaetano Comassi (tenor), Giovanni Ubaldi (tenor).

5. The 1848 Neumane Company (Milan to Lima): Antonio Neumane (impresario, conductor), Lucrezia Micciarelli (soprano, prima donna), Luisa Schieroni (soprano, comprimaria), Rosa Mauri (contralto), Innocenzo Pellegrini (tenor), Luigi Cavedagni (tenor), Luigi Walter (basso), Paolo Borsotti (basso buffo), Felice Ruspini (tenor), Luigi Cavedagni (choir director), Aquila Balicco (stage director), Antonio Meucci (decorations), Luigi Bazzani (costume designer).

6. The 1848 Pantanelli company (Santiago/Valparaiso, Lima and Copiapo): Raffaele Pantanelli (impresario, conductor), Theodore Courtin (concertino), Teresa Rossi, Clorinda Pantanelli, Alessandro Zambaiti, Gaetano Bastoggi, Giovanni Ubaldi, Luigi Grandi, Raffaele Giorgi (decorations).

I will discuss these singers and their journeys in Section 6. The focus of this section will be on how these companies worked, who were the impresarios behind them and how they conducted the business of opera in the Andean region. It would be misleading to define Italian opera companies during the 1840s as 'travelling' troupes. As studied by Katherine Preston, in the United States early opera companies were, often, travelling troupes, featuring a vocal star with a small number of accompanying members. Only later opera companies, with a standard format, became the norm. It was much more difficult to travel with a full company, including all the possible voices for different roles. And even more difficult if one considers a chorus, orchestra and so on. But already in the 1840s, there were large opera companies in the most prestigious and successful opera routes in the Americas, like Havana – New Orleans, or Rio de Janeiro – Buenos Aires. For example, the 1842 New Orleans company, from Havana, included fifty-two members.[86]

---

[86] Katherine Preston, *Opera on the Road: Traveling Opera Troupes in the United States, 1825–60* (University of Illinois Press, 1993), 117.

In comparison, most of the companies working in the Andes during the 1840s and 1850s comprised the bare minimum: two sopranos, one alto, two tenors, one baritone, one buffo and one basso profundo; eight people in total.[87] We can understand such a company, perhaps, in terms of what could be expected for provincial theatres in Italy, rather than the large European venues and capitals that Havana or New Orleans resembled for the New World. In practical terms, in the Andes opera companies were based in one or two big cities at a time, spending a few months on each. The repertoire was between ten and twenty staged operas. They were not based on a single opera star, and often didn't have a star at all.

There were three main impresarios working in the region during this period: Raffaele Pantanelli, Antonio Neumane and Luigi Bazzani. They all came from a musical/theatrical background. Raffaele Pantanelli, a basso,[88] travelled together with his wife Clorinda Corradi to Havana in 1835. Unlike Corradi, he had little success as a singer, and mostly worked to support his wife's outstanding career. Pantanelli worked in Havana for a time as the choir instructor in the famous *Teatro Tacón*. He later conducted opera performances in Peru and Chile, but that was not his original plan: He had to take on the role after the sudden death of Gaetano Guadaroli, the conductor and concertino who arrived with him from Havana. Pantanelli, by several accounts, was the first person in the region to conduct with a baton, rather than from the violin (as Guadaroli did) or from a piano (as Antonio Neumane did).[89] As a footnote, Guadaroli's murder was never fully resolved, but he seems to have been killed after eloping with the daughter of a local medical doctor, Francisco Faustos.[90]

Antonio Neumane had a much more successful musical background for an impresario. After the premiere of his opera *Nicola Terzo*, written while he was still a teenager, the *Allgemeine Musikalische Zeitung* augured a 'brilliant future' for his career.[91] However, he was not able to sustain a career as a composer after that. He appears to have served as accompanist to Maria Malibran during her 1836 visit to Milan, to whom he dedicated one of his finest songs, *Anacreontica*.[92] During the 1830s, Neumane worked as an arranger for Ricordi in Milan. He made at least 350 arrangements of contemporary operas published between 1833 and 1840, including vocal scores for Bellini and Donizetti.[93] He also worked as a teacher, publishing an *Istradamento al*

---

[87] *El Comercio*, Lima, 30 December 1851.
[88] *Corriere degli Spectacoli Italiani*, Bologna, 25 February 1824.
[89] *El Comercio*, Lima, 2 January 1849.   [90] *El Peruano*, Lima, 15 September 1841.
[91] *Allgemeine Musikalische Zeitung*, Leipzig, 20 November 1833.
[92] José Manuel Izquierdo and Álvaro Bravo, *Antonio Neumane: Antología para Canto y Piano* (Ediciones A/B, 2020), 26.
[93] Izquierdo and Bravo, *Antonio Neumane*, 8.

Canto in 1837. Like the Pantanellis, Antonio Neumane and his wife Idalide Turri made their home in South America: after some time in Cuba, he became a central figure in Ecuadorian musical life, writing the national anthem and founding the national conservatoire of Ecuador later in his life.[94]

Luigi Bazzani was another key figure in this period, his career having been studied more recently by Alexander Klein.[95] As a tailor, he was a member of the 1835/6 opera company for Havana, alongside other artists that would later travel to South America during the 1840s, including Clorinda Corradi and Luigi Grandi.[96] Together with Neumane, he arranged for the opera company that performed in Guayaquil in 1842, which included a handful of singers that would become really important for the local music scene, like Paolo Ferretti and Alessandro Zambaiti. Bazzani was a costume designer, and as the owner of costumes and decorations, he was often involved in funding the companies and performances. Bazzani worked together with Pantanelli in Lima after 1842, as well as with Pietro Alessandri, the owner of the Teatro Victoria in Valparaiso, between 1844 and 1846. That year, with the economic support of Alessandri, he served as impresario for a new opera company for Chile and Peru. He travelled to Milan to organize the company with the help of the renowned agent Amato Ricci.[97]

Beyond those impresarios and agents, one should also mention the owners and managers of the theatres, key figures in the business of opera. During late colonial times, theatres had been public institutions, which could be rented to private impresarios in charge of dealing with the performances themselves. Theatres were owned by city councils or public departments closely associated with the management of the city, like hospitals, prisons or cemeteries, and were rented to be managed for a number of years. Their income was key in supporting those other institutions, in particular the hospitals. This continued in Republican times: in 1835, a decree stated that the theatre 'has to be protected by the government, since its profits are used in the support of our hospitals'.[98] Management was also based on strict forms of censorship, prohibition and control, particularly of those kinds of performances that could attract too big an audience.[99] For Juan Pedro Viqueira, who analysed the management of the

---

[94] José Manuel Izquierdo, '"For a Moment, I Felt Like I was Back in Italy": Early South American Experiences of Italian Opera Singers (1840–1860)', in Axel Körner and Paulo Kühl (eds.), *Italian Opera in Global and Transnational Perspective: Reimagining Italianità in the Long Nineteenth Century* (Cambridge University Press, 2021), 137.

[95] Alexander Klein has published a four-volume biography of Luigi Bazzani: *El sastre de dos mundos: Luigi Bazzani y la ópera en América* (Universidad de Los Andes, 2022).

[96] *Teatri, arti e letteratura*, Bologna, 27 August 1835.   [97] *Il Pirata*, Milan, 14 July 1846.

[98] Ricketts, 'El teatro en Lima', 135.   [99] Ricketts, 'El teatro en Lima', 21.

theatre in Lima around the turn of the century, it increasingly looked not only as a form of cultural monopoly, but veritable tyranny.[100]

Some of the managers of these public theatres were key figures in the business of opera during the 1840s and 1850s. In Lima, the Spanish actor Francisco Coya seems to have been one of the most important figures.[101] In Santiago, there were different managers for the old theatre, including Domingo Arteaga.[102] Juan Pablo Izquieta was in charge of the small theatre in Guayaquil.[103] All of them lived through a period of important changes, and made efforts to make theatres more independent from local governments, as well as more profitable for their managers. Already in 1827, Domingo Arteaga was proposing to build a new theatre with a subscription model.[104] And in 1832, in Lima, the violinist Julian Carabayllo tried to convince the members of the Beneficencia, the managers of the old colonial theatre, to effectively 'sell' him the venue, with a lease arrangement for life.[105]

Neither project was successful. The old ways were too ingrained. The model sustained not only other businesses but also local drama companies. Thus, there were many conflicts between theatre managers and opera impresarios. When Raffaele Pantanelli arrived with his company in Lima in 1840, it took weeks for him to arrange a contract with the local theatre. Pantanelli had taken the risk of going to Lima without a previous arrangement, or any knowledge of the region. Local managers were scared of hiring an expensive company that could destroy the budget of the Beneficencia Pública: would there be enough interest in opera, and for how long? The original contract, signed after Pantanelli publicly suggested in the local newspaper that they would depart for Chile if no deal was broken, was for only five performances, one per week for five weeks, plus a benefit concert. For that small trial season, Pantanelli received a rather small amount of 3,000 pesos.[106] The huge success of that original trial season, however, led to almost four years of continuous opera in Lima, and the desire for new companies and new singers to arrive in Peru for the rest of the decade.

The social, cultural and economic success of the Pantanelli company also pushed the desire for new models of theatre management, which would be

---

[100] Juan Pedro Vigueira, '*Relajados o reprimidos': Diversiones públicas y vida social en la ciudad de México durante el siglo de las Luces* (Fondo de Cultura Económica, 1987), 101.

[101] Manuel Moncloa, *Diccionario Teatral del Perú* (Escuela Nacional de Arte Dramático, 2016 [1905]), 55.

[102] Martin Bowen, 'Distraer y gobernar: Teatro y diversiones públicas en Santiago de Chile durante la era de las revoluciones (1780–1836)', *Historia* 49/1 (2016), 27–56.

[103] Pedro José Huerta, *Guayaquil en 1842: Rocafuerte y la epidemia de la fiebre amarilla* (Editorial de la Universidad de Guayaquil, 1987), 28.

[104] Domingo Arteaga, 'La representación dramática que subió al primer grado de esplendor' (published in Santiago de Chile in 1827), 2.

[105] Macera, *Teatro Peruano*, 3.   [106] *El Comercio*, Lima, 8 August 1840.

carried forward in the 1840s and 1850s mainly by foreign businessmen. Pietro Alessandri, whom I previously mentioned, was a key figure and perhaps the first one to successfully develop a new model of theatrical business in the region. An Italian acrobat-turned-entrepreneur who arrived in Chile in the early 1820s, he was the man behind the Teatro Victoria in Valparaiso. In the early 1840s, Alessandri proposed to the city councils of both Santiago and Valparaiso the idea of a fully private theatre, owned and bankrolled by him. He only asked, in return, for an exemption of taxes for fifteen years, during which, he guessed, the venture could become profitable. Santiago rejected the idea, but the city council of Valparaiso supported the motion, not without much debate amongst its members.[107]

After Alessandri's Teatro Victoria, other new theatres were built in the region, a handful of them with private funding. For example, the new theatre in Copiapo, inaugurated in 1848, was built by public subscription. It cost 16,000 pesos.[108] It was a small amount for the small, roofless theatre in the middle of the desert. Around 1850, a French businessman in Lima, Charles Zuderell, became the first one, as far as I know, to build an opera house designed and approved to compete with the 'official', government-sponsored theatre in the same city. The new theatre, called Variedades, would directly vie for the audience of the old Coliseo, by then a run-down building. The impact of the Variedades was such that in 1852 the old Coliseo was bought by the city council of Lima to restore it to its former glory, an important sign of the disruption, but also the innovation caused by the new business models that came with the arrival of Italian opera.[109] But it was commercially sound to build a theatre: five years after its inauguration in 1844, the Victoria was making a profit of 14,000 pesos a year.[110]

Opera had become profitable, but not without effort. For example, these managers had to provide machinery, and technicians, including stage decorators and painters who could provide a tangible theatrical experience. They were mostly foreigners: predominantly Italian and French. As Mariana Lemus as studied for the case of Bogotá, Colombia, people wanted foreign painters as stage designers because they provided an illusion, as one critic put it in 1849: the illusion of forgetting for a moment that 'instead of palaces we have huts ... and in place of public gardens, nothing at all'.[111] Antonio Meucci, for example, arrived in Lima with the Pantanellis, and worked there for a decade as stage

---

[107] Izquierdo, 'The Invention of an Opera House'.
[108] Rodríguez Silva, 'Los orígenes del Teatro en Copiapó', 49.
[109] Rengifo, 'Le théatre historique et la construction de la nation', 81.
[110] *El Mercurio de Valparaiso*, Valparaiso, 24 January 1850.
[111] Mariana Lamus, *Pintores en el escenario teatral* (Universidad del Rosario, 2014), 53.

decorator. In La Paz, in 1846, the central government hired the French painter Paul Lemeteyer to do all the decorations needed for the new theatre.[112] In Valparaiso, Alessandri hired the Bolognese painter Raffaele Giorgi to do the work, and his illusions were often praised in the local newspaper. He was later hired also in Lima, as well as in Buenos Aires, where he was the first stage designer for the old *Teatro Colón*.[113]

People like Coya, Zuderell or Alessandri were directly involved in the business of opera. The success of Italian opera was essential to the profits of their own venues. For example, Francisco Coya, the manager of the old theatre in Lima, led a subscription to hire an opera company to perform in Peru for two years, from 1848 to Carnival of 1850. Officially, Antonio Neumane was the impresario, travelling to Italy, and contacting the singers through the networks of the agent Alberto Torri.[114] But the funding was organized by Coya. Heinrich Witt, a German citizen in Lima, mentions in his diary to have contributed 200 pesos to the enterprise: a year passed between raising the money and the first performances of Verdi's *Ernani* in April 1848.[115]

Pietro Alessandri, in Valparaiso, used his own capital to organize an opera company in Italy in 1846. This time, the man in charge of hiring new singers was Luigi Bazzani. In 1851, Charles Zuderell in Lima did the same arrangement with Bazzani.[116] Thus, Bazzani served as an intermediary, an agent for Alessandri and Zuderell, who was the middleman connecting the Andes with Italian singers, through Italian agents and impresarios. By the early 1850s, Italian newspapers often published advertisements for potential singers willing to go to Chile and Peru, describing the 'excellent payments', but also celebrating those operatic 'colonists' when the companies were officially announced for departure.[117]

It was also possible, albeit if more difficult, to arrange for new singers and new music without having to travel to Italy. Alessandri, Pantanelli, Neumane, Bazzani; they all had contacts in Italy to whom they could write to ask for help. For example, an 1847 letter from Pantanelli in Valparaiso to Alessandro Lanari, the famous impresario in Florence, shows the kind of arrangements that could be provided. Pantanelli asks Lanari's opinion about new operas by Verdi, including Macbeth, since he hasn't heard them and *Ernani* had already proven to be a success in the Andes. More specifically, he asks Lanari to send him

---

[112] Macarena Aguayo, 'Gran función lírica, con los mejores trozos de las óperas modernas: El consumo de la ópera en La Paz durante la Temporada de la compañía Ferreti (1847)', unpublished BA thesis, Pontificia Universidad Católica de Chile (2019).

[113] Izquierdo, 'The Invention of an Opera House', 135.

[114] *Il Pirata*, Milan, 6 December 1847.   [115] Witt, *The Diary of Heinrich Witt*, IV/164.

[116] *El Comercio*, Lima, 30 December 1851.

[117] *Il Pirata*, Milan, 26 February 1852; see also *L'Italia Musicale*, Milan, 28 February 1852.

figurini (costume designs) for Pacini's *Saffo*, and intercede with an agent in Bordeaux, who had the rights of a new opera to be sent and performed in South America.[118] Antonio Neumane also wrote on at least one occasion to Italy to ask for four new operas, as well as a new set of Italian-made costumes for the season of 1853.[119] People like Lanari were essential for these procedures: other names that come forward in contemporary sources are, for example, Alberto Torri and Amato Ricci.[120]

Since 1846, and well into the 1860s, the model for organizing an opera company stayed mostly the same. Every two years, someone went to Italy, or contacted an agent in northern Italy, to organize an opera company between six and twelve people. Bazzani went to Italy in 1846, Neumane did it in 1848 and Bazzani again in 1850/1. It was neither safe nor simple to leave everything behind and travel for at least three months back to Europe to arrange for this, but in an era before the telegraph it was often better to travel to Italy than to wait for the letters to arrive. These trips were not without personal consequences: in 1848 Antonio Neumane left his wife and his children alone in Peru for several months, a dangerous proposition that deeply affected the family, as his daughter remembered in an interview many decades later.[121]

The most essential part of this model, and the one which – I believe – made Italian opera profitable, is that singers were hired to perform, at least, in both Peru and Chile, as contemporary contracts and advertisements in the Italian press show. Lima and Santiago often had the height of the season around August and September, at the beginning of spring. Other cities enjoyed singers in between: Valparaiso, for example, often in the summer or in January and February, when the elite audiences from Santiago and other cities from central Chile decamped en masse to the seaside. If singers arrived by steamer, they arrived from the north, and thus they performed first in Lima. When they arrived by sail, from Brazil or Argentina across the Cape Horn (like Schieroni and Pizzoni in the early 1830s, or Ida Edelvira in the early 1850s), they performed in Chile first.

Impresarios and theatre managers knew that they had to work together to make the trip worthy for singers. For example, Charles Zuderell, the main impresario in Lima, had close contacts to the main impresario in Valparaiso, Pietro Alessandri, which were made possible because of steam networks. Zuderell travelled in 1852 from Lima to Valparaiso to reach an agreement on how to operate the theatres of both cities (and Santiago) in tandem, with the

---

[118] Biblioteca Nazionale Italiana, Florence, Carteggi, Lanari 31/II.

[119] *El Comercio*, Lima, 11 March 1853; *El Mercurio de Valparaíso*, Valparaiso, 28 May 1853.

[120] *Il Pirata*, Milan, 6 December 1847; *L'Italia Musicale*, Milan, 8 April 1854.

[121] *El Telégrafo*, Lima, 14 August 1930.

same opera companies, which became the norm in later decades. These arrangements between theatres concerned only opera companies, not dramatic ones, since those were composed almost solely of local people.[122] This model of exchange and dialogue between impresarios was greatly expanded during the 1850s and 1860s, becoming the foundation for performing circuits until the early twentieth century; not only for Italian opera, but also for circuses, zarzuela and instrumental virtuosos.

4 Repertoires of Italian Opera

Technological advances, and the growing organization of impresarios and managers, meant that Italian opera in the Andes became viable and profitable by the late 1840s. But opera itself, the repertoires and performances, was still shaped by material conditions. The operas that were performed in Latin America, and the Andean region, were defined not exclusively by universal ideas of good music or canonical works, but also on the availability and the talent of singers and musicians, as well as the physical availability and actual playability of scores.

This is important when we picture the growing interest in Italian opera in the Andean region in the context of Italian opera as a global phenomenon during the first half of the nineteenth century. As I have mentioned before, in many ways opera served as the Italian empire of the nineteenth century: it fostered the expansion of the Italian language, people, costumes and ideas, through the materiality and performance of opera. This is most effectively seen in contemporary Italian newspapers dedicated to arts, music and theatre. There, almost every number will have news about operatic performances abroad, often well beyond European borders, with translations of local reviews, selections of letters from impresarios abroad, or poems dedicated to Italian singers throughout the globe. To quote one example, from the editorial introduction of an 1843 review of the opera performances conducted by Neumane in Guayaquil in 1842, published in the *Bazar di Novità artistiche* in Milan: 'we want to show to our readers, how much Italian music is doing to affect the spirit of peoples in faraway places, and the value they put in our artists'.[123] As another article put it more bluntly in 1845: these performances were the best sign that 'our Italian opera is expanding'.[124]

The Andes were most certainly considered an exotic frontier of that operatic expansion, with its own operatic ramifications. The land of the Incas had been, for a long time, a subject of opera itself: for example, the fictional tragedy of

---

[122] *El Comercio*, Lima, 25 June 1852.   [123] *Bazar di novita artistiche*, Milan, 28 June 1843.
[124] *Il Pirata*, Milan, 5 January 1844.

Alonso and Cora, a Spaniard and an Inca princess, had been successfully converted to opera by many composers, including, for example, Bianchi in 1786, Méhul in 1791, Mayr in 1803 (in La Scala), Reynolds in London in 1812, or Mayr again in 1815, with Manuel Garcia in the title role.[125] The Andes were also an important part of contemporary European imagination during the first half of the nineteenth century, considering the popular and successful scientific explorations of, for example, Alexander von Humboldt and Charles Darwin. The image they, and others, produced was of an exotic, foreign land ripe for discoveries, as well as romance, adventure and conquest. Opera could well expand on that market.

But what kind of opera was on the expansion? This question puts the focus not only on the repertoire being performed, but also on how it was performed, and how it was received by local audiences and contemporary local artists. Local, not only in terms of the Andean region; also, in consideration of the subtle differences between the audiences of each city. Newspapers and private documents show that there were divergences. For example, operas that were successful in Lima were not necessarily a furore in Santiago. In 1844, just after arriving in Chile, Clorinda Corradi-Pantanelli wrote in a letter that people in Santiago and Valparaiso seemed much more interested in opera seria, while audiences in Lima preferred opera buffa.[126] There might, in fact, be an explanation for this. In Lima, performances at the time of the arrival of Pantanelli company in 1840 were still decidedly old-fashioned, with Spanish comedies and tonadillas – similar in sound and topics to opera buffa – being the core repertoire. In Chile, however, the famous Argentinian actor, Juan Casacuberta, had been performing since 1842 mostly dramatic roles. By all accounts a wonderful actor, he had put drama in vogue in the Chilean capital: he transformed local taste with some of his performances, like his celebrated *Otello*.[127]

The core repertoire for these operatic companies in the 1840s were the operas by Bellini, Donizetti, and a handful of those by Rossini, in particular *Barbiere* and, more surprisingly, *Tancredi*, whose 'Di tanti palpiti' was still a popular aria at the time in the Andean region. As I previously mentioned, the last operatic performances on stage had been those by Teresa Schieroni and Domenico Pizzoni in the early 1830s, focused on the works of Rossini. Thus, Rossini

[125] José Manuel Izquierdo and Victor Rondon, 'Las canciones patrióticas de José Bernardo Alzedo (1788–1878)', *Revista Musical Chilena* 68/222 (2014), 25.

[126] Letter from Clorinda Corradi, 28 May 1844. In Richert, 'La correspondencia del pintor alemán', 152.

[127] Eugenio Pereira Salas, *Historia del Teatro en Chile: desde sus orígenes hasta la Muerte de Juan Casacuberta* (Ediciones de la Universidad de Chile, 1974), 218.

was still felt as the gold standard, frozen in time for a decade in the local taste. After the premiere of Bellini's *I Capuleti* in Lima, someone wrote: '[back then] we heard Rossini with his *Barbero de Sevilla* and he still has us in awe, open-mouthed . . . he has played all strings for us, while Bellini has, for now, only just played one'.[128] Indeed, it took quite some time for people to fully appreciate the new repertoire of Donizetti and Bellini: in the words of soprano Teresa Rossi, 'their hearts are still cold to these new sensations, but we will get them accustomed'.[129]

Among Donizetti's operas, the most popular ones (at least in terms of the number of performances during the 1840s) were *Lucrezia Borgia*, *Marino Faliero* and *Lucia di Lammermoor*. *Elisir d'Amore* was more popular in Lima than in other places, perhaps because the story and music seem so close to the world of comedies and tonadillas. But it was also performed successfully as a small-scale opera, without a full company, as when Paolo Ferretti and María España performed it in La Paz in 1847.[130] *Anna Bolena* was not performed often, but it had a very powerful and memorable performance when Clorinda Corradi sung it alongside her daughter, Alaide Pantanelli, for Alaide's public debut on the stage in 1847.[131] The epoch-making opera was, however, Bellini's *I Capuleti*, a vehicle for Rossi as Juliet and Corradi as Romeo, performances which were profoundly admired by an entire generation. Other operas by Bellini were never as popular as these two in the Andean region. But Clorinda Corradi herself was often celebrated for her role as Norma in Bellini's opera, the role in which she was painted by Raymond Monvoisin, and in which by all accounts she excelled (see Figure 1). The portrait still hangs in the National History Museum, in Santiago, and was copied by students and amateurs: at least one contemporary copy by a local female painter has also survived.[132]

That was the core repertoire. But many other operas were performed during these years. For example, several lesser-known ones by Donizetti: *Olivo e Pasquale*, *Torquato Tasso*, *Gemma di Vergy* or *Pia di Tolomei,* all of which were performed by the Pantanellis. There were also performances of a few operas by Luigi Ricci, including *Clara di Rosemberg, Chi Dura Vince* and *La Dama Soldato*, none of which were very successful with local audiences. Or at least not as much as *Crispino e la Comare*, a staple of travelling opera

---

[128] *El Comercio*, Lima, 18 September 1840.
[129] Letter from Teresa Rossi, 2 May 1844. In Richert, 'La correspondencia del pintor alemán', 153.
[130] *La Época*, La Paz, 21 September 1847.
[131] *El Mercurio de Valparaíso*, Valparaiso, 6 November 1847.
[132] Emma de Ramón, 'Norma y el desacato: la Sociedad chilena frente a la irrupción de las mujeres artistas (1840–1850)', in *Seminario Historia del Arte y Feminismo* (Museo Nacional de Bellas Artes, 2013), 22–39. www.genero.patrimoniocultural.gob.cl/651/articles-49719_archivo_01.pdf.

Figure 1 Raymond Monvoisin, Clorinda Corradi-Pantanelli as Norma (c.1845)

companies in the Asia-Pacific region during the second half of the century. Verdi only started to gain real fervour in the Andes in 1848, with the arrival of Lucrezia Micciarelli and her performances of *Ernani* in Lima that same year. These performances of Verdi were expanded by *I Due Foscari* in 1849 and *Attila* in 1850. That same year, *Ivanhoe* (*Il Templario*) by Otto Nicolai was also performed, the closest the Andes got to German opera. Carl Maria von Weber, a popular composer in North America,[133] did not circulate in the Andes at this time, either staged or as scores. But there is a long, an unexpected, commentary on Wagner's *Tannhauser* in the frontpage of *El Mercurio de Valparaiso* in 1849, as far as I know the first essay on Wagner published in Latin America.[134] Only in 1851 a French travelling company visited Chile and Peru, performing a completely different repertoire: including, among other operas, *Le Caïd* by Thomas, *La Dame Blanche*, by Boieldieu, or *Le Domino Noir* by Auber. But that is part of a different story.

For local audiences, one of the most shocking aspects of the way the Italian repertoire was performed was the fact that singers were often cross-dressed in trouser roles, in which women performed as men. As Macarena Robledo has

---

[133] Candace Bailey, *Unbinding Gentility: Women Making Music in the Nineteenth-Century South* (University of Illinois Press, 2021), 79.

[134] Hugo Muñoz, 'La recepción discursiva de la figura y obra de Richard Wagner en América Latina durante el siglo XIX', unpublished MA thesis, Pontificia Universidad Católica de Chile (2022).

studied, this was not only abhorred in local reviews of dramatic performances during the 1830s, but also explicitly forbidden by late-colonial law.[135] For Clorinda Corradi, trouser roles were already something of a specialty in her Italian years. In the Andes, she even sang many male roles that were never meant for female singers, like Rodrigo in *Otello* or Edgardo in *Lucia di Lammermoor*, a role for which she became well known. As Macarena Robledo has studied, this led to her being preferred by the audience over the tenors of the company, but it also led to obvious tensions with her male colleagues.[136] For local audiences it took some time to adapt to the fact that these roles worked so well, particularly with Corradi as Romeo in *I Capuleti*. The moral and aesthetic issues of trouser roles were hotly debated in the press. For example, it was a contentious topic in several numbers of *El Comercio* in Lima, during the winter of 1843, when Clorinda had to sing the role usually performed by Zambaiti in *La Sonnambula*, because he was sick: 'if this continues, we will find an upside-down world, where all men will come out dressed as women, and women dressed as men'.[137] Others went even further: 'A judge should put an end to this [travesty].'[138]

It is intriguing, too, that, perhaps, some operas might have been more successful in the Andes than they were in Italy. One case, for example, is *Il Fornaretto* by Gualterio Sanelli. While by no accounts a failure in Italy, it might have been more popular in the Andes than in Italy, particularly in Chile. Its success in Valparaiso was commented on in several Italian newspapers in the early 1850s. Perhaps, it was a tactic by Sanelli himself, to give his opera a second chance of success in Italy.[139] Each new opera, however successful in Italy, could mean a financial risk for an Italian company in the Andes, since it was impossible to know beforehand how local audiences would react to it. A collection of posters and leaflets announcing opera performances in the 1840s and 1850s is preserved in the Biblioteca Nacional de Chile. It is not unusual for those presenting new operas to have paragraphs like this one:

> The company wants to announce that this new opera [*Il Giuramento*, by Mercandante] is in no way less interesting than the popular *Lucrezia* and the sentimental *Ernani*: the composer is admired, with justice, as the wisest of modern composers, and among his operas this one is the most popular abroad. Who has not felt pleasure with Victor Hugo's *Angelo*? And what if we also add the sublime performances of Rossi and Pantanelli? It suggests a huge success.[140]

---

[135] Macarena Robledo is currently studying this problem for her unpublished MA thesis on the Pontificia Universidad Católica de Chile, and I'm grateful for her suggestion.

[136] *El Comercio*, Lima, 7 July 1843.   [137] *El Comercio*, Lima, 27 June 1843.

[138] *El Comercio*, Lima, 30 June 1843.   [139] *Gazetta Musicale di Milano*, Milan, 2 April 1854.

[140] This document is found in the Biblioteca Nacional de Chile, in a collection of loose theatrical documents, under location LCH47-48.

Much work was done through newspapers to support the performance of these new operas in a different language. José Santos Tornero, the editor of *El Mercurio de Valparaíso*, printed a magazine titled *El Mensajero del Teatro Victoria*, which was sold before new performances. It was mainly directed towards Spanish-speaking readers, rather than the huge community of European immigrants in Valparaiso. The range of topics inside the magazine was extensive, but mostly focused on addressing new and underperformed operas, explaining their historical context, the technique of certain composers, or the differences between the literary and historical sources and the libretto. Operatic news from around the globe was also published, fostering the notion that the Andean operatic scene was part of a larger, integrated world of operatic performances, peoples and venues.[141]

For each new opera, a libretto was translated and printed: Italian on one page and Spanish on the opposite side. In Lima, libretti were printed by José Masías, while in Chile by José Santos Tornero, clearly an opera-lover who, in his memoires, wrote much about this period of operatic history.[142] Selling libretti, of course, was also good business for printers, as Laura Suárez has studied for the case of Mexico in the 1840s.[143] Libretti are also good sources, today, to understand which parts of the operas were cut, or if important changes were made. For example, the libretto of Donizetti and Romani's *Parisina* (printed in 1844 in Valparaiso) includes different words for the Duetto in scene 7 between Parisina and Ugo. It was taken from act three of *I normanni a Parigi*, an 1832 opera with words by the same Romani, but music by Mercadante.[144] Translators are rarely mentioned, but we know of a few names, like the poet and politician Hermógenes de Irisarri and the left-wing writer Jacinto Chacón, who were the authors of some of those translations.[145]

The fact that libretti often point us towards important changes in the structure of the operas, as was often the case in this period, also begs the question for music performed, and the quality of performances. Local musicians often praised music performances. The clarinettist José Zapiola, for example, wrote in his memoirs that the orchestra, as conducted by Pantanelli, rarely made a mistake.[146] Foreign travellers often were more critical. For example, Jakob

---

[141] Izquierdo, 'The Invention of an Opera House', 145.

[142] José Santos Tornero, *Reminiscencias de un Viejo editor* (Imprenta de la librería del Mercurio, 1889).

[143] Laura Suárez, 'Los libretos: un negocio para las imprentas. 1830–1860', in Laura Suárez (ed.), *Los Papeles para Euterpe: la Música en la ciudad de México desde la Historia Cultural, siglo XIX* (Instituto de Investigaciones Dr. José María Luis Mora, 2014), 100–42.

[144] The libretto in Spanish is preserved in the Biblioteca Nacional de Chile, 9;(145–31). I am grateful to Macarena Robledo for pointing out this detail in the libretto.

[145] Izquierdo, 'The Invention of an Opera House', 148.

[146] José Zapiola, Recuerdos de treinta años (El Independiente, 1874), 96.

Tschudi wrote that, beyond the lack of theatrical machines, historically appro-
priate costumes and a good supporting choir, 'orchestras leave much to be
desired'.[147] Of course, this was not the same everywhere: according to
Clorinda Corradi, for example, 'the orchestra in Santiago is much better than
the one in Lima, which allows us to rehearse twice the number of operas'.[148] In
general, one can imagine that the level was rather poor, since there are several
accounts of operas, even overtures, being stopped midway because of the lack
of coordination.[149] Beyond the early lack of familiarity with the repertoire,
a reason for the low orchestral level might have been the fact that musicians
were gathered from several different backgrounds. String players often came
from local churches, but the winds came from military bands.[150] Wind players
were often the most criticized, being pitied by reviewers; one solo player was
bad enough to 'shake the theatre'.[151]

In terms of the actual music being performed, it was very common to make
reductions and orchestrations. The Biblioteca Nacional del Perú preserves
a good collection of orchestral scores from this period, sadly still not fully
catalogued or publicly available, which shows the enormous amount of changes
music had to suffer to be performed. For example, parts for *Belisario* and *Lucia
di Lammermoor* show a very different orchestration from the original one, as
well as important structural differences, with large sections being cut.[152]
Orchestral parts for *Norma*, apparently performed in Arequipa, include
a 'Casta Diva' with the flute solo written for the cello.[153] An important reason
for these changes was economic: it was not always convenient to hire a full
orchestra, and thus often parts were cut, particularly wind parts like the brass or
oboes, as Antonio Neumane did for the operatic performances of the season of
1851 in Santiago.[154] The inability of certain players to perform some of the
pieces also needed to be considered.

Another factor in those orchestrations was the lack of full orchestral scores,
and there are clear signs in contemporary sources that much of the repertoire
was performed at least in part from newly orchestrated versions of vocal piano
scores. For example, when Paolo Ferretti went to perform with a company of his
own to La Serena (in the north of Chile) in 1858, he wrote to Isidora Zegers,
a celebrated *salonniere* and amateur soprano, to ask her for vocal scores of

---

[147] Tschudi, *Peru: Reiseskizzen*, 120.
[148] Letter from Clorinda Corradi, 28 May 1844. In Richert, 'La correspondencia del pintor alemán',
       152.
[149] *El Comercio*, Lima, 10 December 1844.   [150] *La Época*, La Paz, 17 November 1845.
[151] *El Mercurio de Valparaíso*, Valparaiso, 11 and 23 January 1845.
[152] Biblioteca Nacional del Perú, nineteenth-century manuscripts collection, C2P2.
[153] Biblioteca Nacional del Perú, nineteenth-century manuscripts collection, C60P327.
[154] Eugenio Pereira Salas, *Historia de la Música en Chile 1850–1900* (Editorial Universitaria, 1950), 18.

'[Rossini's] Mosè in Egitto and [Mozart's] Don Giovanni, to stage and orchestrate some sections'.[155] Italian opera also circulated as vocal scores, piano arrangements or as part of the repertoire of military brass bands, a staple of the nineteenth-century urban soundscape. In many cases, operas were known to local audiences first as reductions, and only later in a staged format. The borders between what was considered 'original' or 'authentic' and what was not, were blurry.[156]

One aspect that defines opera in Latin America during this period is the almost complete lack of new works composed by local artists, for local audiences. It was the success of Melesio Morales' *Ildegonda*, premiered in Mexico in 1866 and performed in Florence in 1869, and later of Carlos Gomes' *Il Guarany* in Milan, in 1870, that opened the gates for Latin American operas. Until then, there had been very few exceptions: Manuel Covarrubias premiered *Reynado y Elina* in Mexico, in 1838. *Tonadillas*, however, were still very popular in some cities, and pieces by Atanasio Bello Montero or José María Osorio in Venezuela, as well as Pedro Ximénez Abrill in Perú, do survive.[157] But operas, in the style and with the influence and cultural weight of Italian operas, were almost non-existent until the 1860s; and those that might have existed were not performed.

In the Andean region, the situation was not different, but there were some tantalizing projects during the 1840s that could have come to fruition. For example, a libretto survives titled *The Ruin of Callao*, for an opera in three acts written in English, and published in Lima in 1847, anonymously. According to the preface, the first act of the opera was printed in 'a late English paper published in Lima', but the second was delayed and the third never appeared: the libretto was printed to search for a composer who never arrived. The opera consists of 'songs' and spoken parts, with five principal characters apart from officers, friars and women. There is a love story, but the tragedy lurks behind: the 1746 earthquake that destroyed Lima and shocked the port of El Callao with a tsunami, gives the context for the play. Indeed, the most important scene must be the final one, with the musical imitation of the earthquake, the 'rushing waters', followed by the survival of the protagonist Lorenzo only to find, through the voices of a solemn, invisible choir, that her love, Azelia, was swept by the ocean. Central to the libretto, the author states, is not only the love story and the tragedy, but the contradictions between the 'supernatural', religion and the 'progress of natural science'.[158]

---

[155] Letter from Ferretti to Isidora Zegers, 26 June 1858. Archivo Central Andrés Bello, Chile.

[156] Izquierdo, 'Rossini's Reception in Latin America'.

[157] Izquierdo, 'El Militar retirado de Pedro Jiménez'; Montserrat Capelán, 'La tonadilla escénica en Venezuela'.

[158] *The Ruin of Callao, in 1746: An Opera in Three Acts* (Oficinas del C`omercio, 1847).

The other project from the period for which we have some documentation is Aquinas Ried's opera, *La Telésfora*, for which he wrote both the music and a libretto, in Spanish, in 1846. Born in 1809 in Aberdeen, Scotland, as James Aquinas Reid, he worked there as an organist, and later studied to become a medical doctor in Germany. He had a somewhat successful career as a composer in Scotland: according to several sources, an oratorio by him based on Milton's *Paradise Lost* was premiered in Glasgow.[159] He departed for Australia, an organist in Sydney, where he premiered a Mass and sections from an opera, before moving to the island of Norfolk. In 1844 he departed Australia towards Valparaiso, where he presented himself as Aquinas Ried, a German citizen, to escape a possible conviction back in Norfolk. Most of Ried's music has been lost, his manuscripts destroyed during the bombing of Valparaiso by the Spanish armada in 1866. But the libretto for *La Telesfora*, printed for the premiere, still survives.

Ried/Reid had very practical notions on how to compose an opera for the available local conditions: he admired Clorinda Corradi, who became the protagonist of his opera, as Telesfora. As he put it in a letter to Isidora Zegers in 1868, however, the lack of good choirs and a good orchestra were always a consideration for him when writing his music. He wrote two more operas, neither of which made it to the stage. The Pantanelli company rehearsed *Telesfora* in late 1846, but ten days before the premiere, the opera was cancelled.[160] There are two possible reasons: one is that the opera was not working for the voices in the company; the other is that Ried had to leave Valparaiso for a new job in Bolivia.

An 'heroic opera' in three acts, as he puts it, *Telesfora* considers six main characters: two Spanish, two Chilean and two Mapuche, Indigenous people from Chile:

Pelayo	A Chilean patriot	José Martí
Gonzalvo	A Spanish realist	Alessandro Zambaiti
Lincoyan	Head [Cacique] of the Mapuche	Nestor Corradi
Auca	Son of Lincoyan	Juditta Ricci
Telesfora	Widow, sister-in-law of Pelayo	Clorinda Corradi
Irene	Telesfora's daughter	Teresa Rossi

---

[159] José Manuel Izquierdo, 'Totaleindruck o impresión total: La Telésfora de Aquinas Ried como proyecto político, creación literario-musical, reflejo personal y encuentro con el otro', *Revista Musical Chilena* 65/215 (2011), 5–22.

[160] Izquierdo, 'Totaleindruck o impresión total', 9.

The libretto of the opera is well constructed, balancing the three layers of characters and using the plot to build a sense of common national identity that is not there at the beginning of the opera. The inclusion of important roles for Indigenous people has to be noted, not only because it anticipates later developments of Latin America and the interest in exotic local elements (like Gomes' *Il Guarany*), but also because of Ried's own involvement with Indigenous causes in Chile at a time when there were growing calls for the occupation and destruction of Indigenous lands and peoples. In fact, concerned about the possible military invasion of the Indigenous southern lands, he travelled there to know first-hand the situation of some communities in the south of Chile.[161] This very personal preoccupation comes through in the roles of Lincoyan and Auca, central to the second act of the opera.

In the opera, Irene is the main love interest, as performed by Teresa Rossi, but the real agency is with Clorinda Corradi's Telesfora. The role of Telesfora, and the relationship between the characters, are clearly modelled on Norma, but there are also prominent fantastic elements in the opera, which might very well be connected to a connection with contemporary German romantic opera. The last act was likely modelled on Bellini's *Norma*, but it might also include elements of Verdi's *Giovanna d'Arco*, premiered only two years before *Telesfora* and known then through vocal scores. Telesfora, like Norma, summons a group of Chilean patriots, lazily singing around a campfire, to go to war against Spain. She takes their guitar, throws it to the fire and sings: 'Are you not ashamed that a woman has to call you to arms?' Telesfora's last aria turns, surprisingly, into the Chilean national anthem, taken up[?] by the choir of soldiers and calls to arms.

For people in the audience, many of whom had lived through the Wars of Independence, it would have been a stirring moment. It is well known that in European opera, the chorus could often serve as a form of collective political representation of the nation: the idea of the chorus as representing 'a people whose political destiny is central to the dramatic action'.[162] But, as far as I know, no European opera has such a blunt way of forcing a political reading as the actual singing of the national anthem in the climactic scene of *Telesfora*. In Italy, in particular, national sentiments are often sublimated, the choir representing foreign or historical groups of people, rather than contemporary ones, as for example in Verdi's *I Lombardi* or *Nabucco*. And, in Chile, that

---

[161] Izquierdo, 'Totaleindruck o impresión total', 12–13.

[162] James Parakilas, 'Political Representation and the Chorus in the Nineteenth-Century Opera', *19thCentury Music* 16/2 (1992), 181–202. See also from Susan Rutherford, 'Crime and Punishment: Tales of the Opera Chorus in Nineteenth-Century Parma', *Nineteenth Century Theatre and Film* 33/2 (2006), 1–11.

music, if premiered, would have been listened with a deep connection between past and presence, with obvious national overtones that could only be dreamed of in Italy at the time.

5 The Limits of Italian Opera

One of the most difficult tasks when dealing with opera in this period is to ascertain how popular, how successful it really was. It is easy to think that Italian opera was mostly an elite affair, promoted by local aristocracies. That was up to a point true in some cities, like Valparaiso, where the elite was composed of European migrants who appreciated opera as a way to connect with their homelands on the other side of the Atlantic. However, it was not necessarily the case for other large cities, like Lima and Santiago, where a Catholic elite seemed entrenched in conservative colonial practices, and thus opera first gained ground within the middle classes.

More importantly, Italian opera had to compete with many other forms of entertainment, which had catered to different social groups. With the disappearance of *tonadillas* and sung comedias from the repertoire after the permanent settlement of Italian opera in the Andes in the early 1840s, there were no other forms of theatrical musical entertainment that could truly compete with it. Only by the 1850s would travelling companies of other kinds of musical theatre (including Spanish zarzuela) become central to the Latin American and Asia-Pacific theatrical, operatic and performing scenes. But the lack of competition from similar genres does not mean that opera had no competition from other forms of entertainment. And it is against that competition, that also the very local differences in the reception of Italian opera also become evident.

Early reception of Italian opera in the Andes confronts us with some of the borderlines of considering opera, essentially, as a form of drama. In Chile, the early reception of the Pantanelli company was in large part shaped by its comparison to drama. Argentinian actor Juan Casacuberta arrived in Chile in 1841, quickly becoming a star who popularized drama in a romantic vein. And, because Casacuberta's company was not a stable, local one, it was possible for him to interact in a different way with opera singers. For example, he brought Paolo Ferretti and María España during his seasons in Lima and Arequipa in 1846. This favoured a more nuanced relation between drama and opera that was also extended to contemporary discussions. One of the best essays on this topic came after the first performance of *I Capuleti* in Santiago, written by Domingo Faustino Sarmiento, the celebrated Argentinian writer:

> When listening to opera for the first time, what strikes the spirit is how improper
> it looks to have everyday scenes performed in song [*representar* cantando],

as if melody could reshape drama and tragedy. ... People say that one should leave common sense behind to really appreciate opera, but it seems to me that, on the contrary, one should bring in an appreciation of the arts; a consciousness that subordinates reason itself. ... Drama can be shaped by many forms of art, including painting, sculpture, and the word, but also music, the voice, and instruments. ... Drama uses the action and the words to paint passions, ideas, and sentiments; but opera takes sounds to arrive at the same object, and they certainly seem to be wonderful tools to express the truth and the strength of our souls. So, for those who ask: Where have you seen people crying or dying while singing? I could say: Where have you seen men of stone, bronze, or wood? Opera seems to me only inferior to drama, in that there is sometimes no correlation between activity and feeling. Words in drama go as fast as the passions it paints; but, when combined with sound, the same cannot happen in opera. ... The action, thus, is easily hindered by the music and quickly becomes languid. If not for that caveat, opera would be equal to drama, given that it is certainly superior in its capacity to manifest tender passions and popular scenes where a chorus can represent the individuality and togetherness of a human group.[163]

But, for the rest of this section, I would like to focus on Lima, where the reception of opera was much more difficult, and where the limits of a successful operatic reception were much more obvious. The most direct adversaries of Italian opera were drama companies and dramatic actors, who had been a staple of local stages, performing in Spanish, since colonial times. The guilds of actors felt that opera was an unfair competition to them, and one which drastically affected the way local governments, theatre managers and the audiences related to stage artists. The pressure of local drama companies was often felt when opera singers arrived in new places. Different members of the cultural world feared opera's capacity to disrupt local practices, and therefore local jobs. This can be seen already in 1831, when the opera company led by Domenico Pizzoni and Teresa Schieroni arrived in Lima, and there were discussions at the level of the city council, about the role the government had to play in supporting opera: the idea was that, while opera could make money on its own, local funding should go always first to 'national artists', in particular dramatic actors, over members of the 'lyric company'.[164]

More than two decades later, in 1855, there were still signs of that same protectionism: when composer José Bernardo Alzedo proposed the creation of a national conservatoire in Lima, his argument was, again, that local artists should be preferred over foreign ones, given that, in his opinion, so many Italian singers only cared about 'making a fortune with which to return to their

---

[163] *El Progreso*, Santiago, 23 April 1844.
[164] Archivo General de la Nación, Lima, RPJ 428, 10: 87.

homeland'.[165] This notion, of protection against the influx of Italian opera and Italian performers, understood as a powerful foreign power that consumed local resources, and against which local artists could not compete, has to be considered in all its seriousness. In 1847, when a small opera company led by Paolo Ferretti arrived in La Paz, Bolivia, the actors of the dramatic company wrote to the government asking for several privileges, including that no 'foreign company' should be allowed to perform in the theatre during their seasons.[166]

In Lima, the situation was even worse. The same month that the Pantanelli company arrived in Lima, in August 1840, there were important discussions in the theatre about the protection of the dramatic company, and much gossip in newspapers about possible price increases of tickets, caused by opera. Someone even published that, if the Italian opera company was allowed to perform, the dramatic company would be dissolved, and that Limeños would have no entertainment when the Italians left since the drama company was the only national and 'permanent' one.[167] During the next months, and years, there were often discussions about the role of drama in an age of opera: 'opera has made us forget that drama exists . . . but spoken drama can be sometimes as interesting as the sung one'.[168] And, in fact, by 1843, there was no drama company in Lima, making it impossible for them to compete against its 'antagonist', Italian opera.[169]

But the idea of the drama company being a 'national' one was at least partially an exaggeration. In 1840, when the Pantanellis arrived, the drama company in Lima was in fact led by Carlo Fedriani, an Italian actor, who managed it with financial support from the government.[170] But just a week after the Pantanellis arrived, Fedriani, alongside the celebrated actress Carmen Aguilar, left for Ecuador. This timely escape was hotly debated, since so many interpreted their departure as a sign of retreat and capitulation.[171] They departed to inaugurate a new theatre in Guayaquil on 20 August 1840; the same venue in which the Neumane company performed in 1842.[172] It seems symptomatic, however, that Fedriani returned from Guayaquil two years later, in May 1842.[173] He only resumed his performances on the Limenian stage in May 1844, a few weeks after the Pantanellis left for Chile.[174] And even then,

[165] Biblioteca Nacional del Perú, a copy is preserved in the Colección Carlos Raygada.
[166] Archivo y Bibliotecas Nacionales de Bolivia, MIP, T7: N34. I am grateful to Macarena Aguayo for this.
[167] *El Comercio*, Lima, 13 August 1840.   [168] *El Comercio*, Lima, 30 September 1840.
[169] *El Comercio*, Lima, 30 June 1843; see also 22 July 1843.
[170] *El Peruano*, Lima, 24 May 1840.   [171] *El Comercio*, Lima, 11 August 1840.
[172] José Joaquín Olmedo, *Obras poéticas de D. José Joaquín Olmedo* (Imprenta Europea, 1848), 132.
[173] *El Comercio*, Lima, 14 May 1842.   [174] *El Comercio*, Lima, 11 May 1844.

there were explicit comments in the press about the 'bitter pill' opera had been for the drama company, as well as the vengeance Fedriani took against any solitary opera singers who had stayed behind in Lima and wanted to perform arias alongside the drama company.[175]

It is true, however, that beyond Fedriani, Lima had a long tradition of actors and actresses, and many of them, as I have mentioned before, had trained in the tradition of comedias and the Spanish *tonadilla*. This training allowed them to perform popular songs and short musical numbers on the stage, but not full operas. Many of the most prominent artists in Lima during the first half of the nineteenth century gained their popularity through tonadillas, like Fernando Bull, Fernanda Varamendi, Petronila Figueroa or the celebrated Rosa Merino, who sang Rossini on a handful of occasions during the 1820s. Carmen Aguilar, the Peruvian actress working with Fedriani, for example, followed those steps, as singer, actress and producer, but performers like her could not compete, in technical terms, with the newly arrived Italian opera singers, something that had already been obvious with the opera performances of 1812 and 1831.

But the most direct competition to opera was not dramatic theatre or the old-school tonadillas, but bullfighting. Lima was a city that 'among those in South America, might be the most faithful to the old Spanish customs', as someone wrote in 1843.[176] The conservative Catholic elite in Lima was not as comfort-able in watching opera and often decried it in contemporary Catholic journals. Specific details about attendances are scarce, but both Pablo Macera in 1991 and Monica Ricketts in 1996 recovered suggestive documents while going through the uncatalogued Archivo de la Beneficencia de Lima. For example, numbers of tickets sold in 1831 and 1840, respectively, show that Italian opera greatly increased attendance in the theatre, but not in all sections of the theatre. The pit and the upper rings[?], were full, but boxes either stayed the same or declined in numbers, meaning that, at least in the beginning, opera was less successful with Lima elites.[177]

The most popular form of entertainment, for the elite, was bullfighting. A comparison between opera and bullfighting, strange as it might seem to us today, was one made repeatedly by people in Lima in the 1840s. However, we should remember, Italian opera and bullfighting are indeed close siblings, and that relationship was reinforced during the nineteenth century. Both have medieval origins, affected by a sixteenth-century interest in the partial redis-covery of classical forms of arts and entertainment: Greek in opera, Roman in bullfighting. In the case of Lima, the Plaza de Acho, the bullfighting arena, was

---

[175] *El Comercio*, Lima, 7 June 1844.

[176] Max Radiguet, *Lima y la sociedad peruana* (Biblioteca Nacional del Perú, 1971 [1841]), 3.

[177] Macera, *Teatro Peruano*, 40; Ricketts, 'El teatro en Lima', 146.

built in 1766, the same period in which the theatre had been raised. With a capacity for more than 10,000 people, the Plaza de Acho, however, still exists. Theatre and bullfighting were developed in tandem in Lima during this period, both being seen as colonial tools for propaganda, social control and education. Theatre and bullfighting were key pillars for the funding of public institutions, particularly hospitals. They complemented each other: one being the entertainment for the day, the other for the night.

Bullfighting was then, as now, a key event for the Limenian elite. But for European travellers it was always depicted as a symbol of the barbaric, the non-civilized in the old Spanish capital of South America. While one European writer comments on 'the cruelty of the sport',[178] another does so about the 'barbarous diversions [that are] a national disgrace'.[179] Another wrote of the torment that 'take away all pleasure in the spectacle from persons not habituated to such sights',[180] and the general consensus from travellers is that bullfighting, like slavery before it, had to disappear for the city to truly become modern. With the arrival of opera, performances by the Pantanelli company became the needed symbol to finally confront bullfighting with something perceived as the opposite model. As one European traveller wrote at the time, there was hope that opera would be able to finally 'overcome the national amusement of the bull-fight'.[181]

This dualism is made explicit by the German painter Moritz Rugendas, a good friend of the Pantanellis (with whom he lived at least for some time in Lima), in his painting *The Square of Lima*, from 1843. It depicts Lima's main square as the background for distinct social stereotypes. Men of the upper classes survey the different groups, from 'tapadas' (women with covered faces) to freed slaves and poor children. Europeans and white citizens are portrayed on the left side of the painting, while mulattoes and those of the lower classes are distinctly portrayed on the right side. Correspondingly, there is an advertisement for European opera on a pillar on the left (Bellini's *I Capuleti*, with Rossi and Corradi), and one for bullfighting on the right, which were not originally in any of the sketches Rugendas made, and thus can be thought as very conscious element (see Figure 2).[182]

---

[178] William Ruschenberger, *Three Years in the Pacific: Containing Notices of Brazil, Chile, Bolivia, Peru* (Richard Bentley, 1835), 146.

[179] Tschudi, *Peru: Reiseskizzen*, 155.   [180] Hall, *Extracts from a Journal*, 101.

[181] Robinson Warren, *Dust and Form of Three Oceans and Two Continents* (Charles Scribner, 1859), 13–14.

[182] A reproduction from an early sketch can be found in the collections of the Biblioteca Nacional de Chile: www.bibliotecanacionaldigital.gob.cl/bnd/632/w3-article-314055.html. Another sketch, including the reference to bullfighting, is preserved in the Museo de Arte de Lima: https://

Figure 2 Moritz Rugendas, La Plaza Mayor de Lima (c.1843)

In 1843, the same year Rugendas painted his view of Lima, a bullfighting season was dedicated to the wife of then president/dictator of Peru Manuel Ignacio de Vivanco.[183] Very expensive bulls were presented for several weeks in June and July, when the opera company was performing *Belisario* and *La Donna del Lago*.[184] Bullfighting, like theatre and opera, was announced with *listines*, leaflets that were given by boys accompanied by a band of musicians, followed closely by a person who recited allegorical verses printed on the leaflet itself. The ones printed for the bullfighting season of 1843 are striking in that they focus on this growing rift with Italian opera, and critics' attitudes towards both forms of entertainment. I quote:

> Let others sing Norma and Juliet, Belisario and Romeo . . . I would not spend a dime on their voices. I, a poet and no canary sing to the bulls, who are my pleasure, my enthusiasm, and my pride; a show that is both fitting and philharmonic in its own way. And they call it atrocious! What foolishness! But is it not Romeo who dies, and Marino who loses his wife, a victim of destiny? And they say there is nothing horrible about that.[185]

The opposite argument can be found a few weeks later in the local newspaper *El Comercio*, in which a long article discussed the issue of 'Opera and Bulls':

---

artsandculture.google.com/asset/study-for-lima%E2%80%99s-main-square/kAHxHbqppKf7ug?hl=en.

[183] Ricardo Dávalos, *Lima de antaño: cuentos y tradiciones, críticas literarias, artículos de costumbres y de índole narrativa* (Montaner y Simón, 1925), 34.

[184] *El Comercio*, Lima, 13 June 1843.   [185] Radiguet, *Lima y la sociedad peruana*, 54.

'The two only forms of entertainment which can attract audiences in Lima today ... are of such separate nature ... that I hesitate to put them in the same line: Italian opera and bullfighting.' In the pit, there was 'the fastidious smell of blood, or the deep cries of the bulls being mortally hurt', that could not be compared to 'the echo of the works of the trinity of men that are masters in harmony: Rossini, Bellini, Donizetti'.[186] What is striking about both statements, whether in favour or in opposition to bullfighting, is that the problem is presented as a dichotomy as if one couldn't appreciate one alongside the other. So, perhaps the main question here is in which ways bullfighting might have been read by contemporaries in dialogue with opera.

Unlike a theatre, bullfighting is performed in an arena, surrounded by a circular set of stalls and a gallery, in daylight. Audience reactions, however, were very similar to those in opera and theatre, with moments of relative silence being cut by abrupt explosions of noise, applause and cries from the participants. What is perhaps less well known is that music was as central to bullfighting as it was in opera. The centrality of music was determined as much by its role in signposting the dramatic structure as it was because of the physical disposition of musicians inside the bullring. In Lima, there were two military bands underneath the president's box, chosen each time from the dozen or so in the city. Reviewers sometimes commented on the bands, one from 1856 complaining that it was trying so hard that they seemed to be, I quote, 'competing with the orchestra of the theatre'.[187] The convergence makes sense: musicians from military bands, as I mentioned previously, often joined the ranks of theatre orchestras, to reinforce the wind sections. And operatic selections, as in many other places, were part of the core repertoire of many of those bands. Thus, it would be easy to imagine that they played selections from operas while in the bullfighting arena, reinforcing the connection between both forms of entertainment.

In the collection of nineteenth-century musical manuscripts in the Biblioteca Nacional de Lima, alongside opera arrangements for the theatre, one can also find arrangements for military bands. For example, one album from 1848, for the Second Batallion of Lima (which often performed in the arena at this time), includes not only the overture of *Anna Bolena* but also a suite on arias from *I Capuleti*, that much-celebrated opera as a vehicle for Rossi and Corradi-Pantanelli.[188] Projecting the connection between opera and bullfighting, the most intriguing find in those albums are three different versions of the choir of the bullfighters, the *matadores* from *Traviata*, most probably copied in the late 1850s.

---

[186] *El Comercio*, Lima, 25 July 1843.   [187] *El Comercio*, Lima, 7 April 1856.
[188] Biblioteca Nacional del Perú, part of the uncatalogued nineteenth-century music collection.

The number was significant for Spanish audiences, being the most applauded during the premiere of *Traviata* in Madrid.[189] Also, as Emilio Sala proposed, it has a strong similarity to *El Jaleo de Jerez*, a popular song and dance that is also often found in Peruvian sources of the period, performed both in the theatre and by military bands.[190]

There were other ways, too, in which opera was directly influencing bullfighting. In 1848, encouraged by the recent success of the Italian company led by Lucrezia Micciarelli, the managers from the bullfighting arena, the Plaza de Acho, José María Urresti and José de Asín, decided to hire a company of *matadores* from Spain for the summer bullfighting season.[191] That they followed operatic models is obvious in the way the artists are announced, as well as in grouping them as a 'company' rather than as individual performers, as it was usually done in bullfighting. The group, including Carlos Rodríguez as *primera espada*; and Antonio Romero as *segunda espada*, plus three *banderilleros*, came in the Spanish ship *Perseverancia*, getting off the ship in Callao dressed, according to the newspaper, in 'rigorous *majo* style'.[192] For some reviewers, the visit of a company of Spanish bullfighters was nothing more than 'a step backwards' in terms of the modern Independence of Peru,[193] while for others it was an affront to 'national *toreros*', which Peru did have, unlike Italian singers, echoing the complaints from dramatic actors.[194] Others, however, celebrated the quality of the show, from its foreign costumes to the dangers sustained by the Spanish artists: it was, according to one reviewer, a chance for Lima to be again 'as enthusiastic about bullfighting [as we are] about the sounds of the beautiful Micciarelli'.[195]

In later decades, Italian opera would sustain ample competition from other forms of entertainment too: French companies (the first one visited in 1851), and most obviously from Spanish zarzuela. French opera was never a true competitor, as it was in the Caribbean region, but zarzuela was a much more dangerous affair. The first zarzuela companies arrived during the 1850s, using the business model and the routes of Italian opera companies, usurping their market. When the first zarzuelas were presented to the Lima audience, there was even fear of praising them in case 'our Italian singers, who have worked so hard for their audience, might feel betrayed'.[196] The premiere of Arrieta's *El Dominó Azul* was found to be 'rather a full opera, with original and smart music'.[197]

---

[189] Víctor Sánchez, *Verdi y España* (Ediciones Akal, 2014).
[190] Emilio Sala, *The Sounds of Paris in Verdi's La Traviata* (Cambridge University Press, 2013), 79.
[191] Héctor López, *Plaza de Acho: Historia y Tradición* (Fondo Editorial del Congreso del Perú, 2005), 113.
[192] *El Comercio*, Lima, 30 December 1848.   [193] *El Comercio*, Lima, 2 January 1849.
[194] *El Comercio*, Lima, 10 January 1849.   [195] *El Comercio*, Lima, 29 January 1849.
[196] *El Comercio*, Lima, 24 October 1856.   [197] *El Comercio*, Lima, 20 January 1857.

Zarzuela was read and appreciated in the terms set by Italian opera, thus deeply upsetting the success and prestige of Italian opera. In the opinion of another reviewer: 'it seems like opera, sung and performed in our own language, has enough power [*potencia*] to overthrow opera in a language that even learned audiences don't fully comprehend'.[198] It was a successful prediction: Italian opera was still truly relevant during the second half of the nineteenth century in all Andean cities, but from the 1860s on the economic competition from zarzuela companies became a constant. More importantly, after the arrival of zarzuela, Italian opera never again had the monopoly it carried during the 1840s, when it became, by far, the most prestigious format of musical theatre in urban Andean centres. By the end of the nineteenth century, it is fair to say that zarzuela had outgrown Italian opera in popularity, in its social reach, as well as in opening a real possibility for local creation.

6 A Very Personal Journey

In previous sections, I have shown that Italian opera was a disruptive cultural force in the Andean region, set against a background of several forms of music theatre and public entertainment. It was difficult to push Italian opera into a new frontier, and its adoption by local audiences was in no way granted at the time. And I have also shown that the actions of different people, including impresarios and members of the audience, were key in both its success and its failures. But we are still missing some of the key agents in this process: the singers themselves. Why did singers come to the Andean region? What were their expectations? Why did so many settle to live in the Andes for the rest of their lives? The human dimension of opera, and the very personal journeys of singers, in particular, are a key factor in the success of Italian opera during this period, but also in its long-term cultural impact.

Consider an example: The tenor and impresario Paolo (or Pablo) Ferretti died in Ica, a small oasis in the middle of the Peruvian desert, on the first day of April 1889. He was seventy-nine years old, working there as 'music teacher', widower of Peruvian soprano María España.[199] He had lived in the Andes since 1842, when he arrived with Antonio Neumane as part of the company that gave the first operatic performances in Guayaquil, Ecuador. He was one of the first to perform opera in many other Andean cities, including Concepción in Chile, La Paz in Bolivia, Arequipa in Peru and Quito in Ecuador, where he premiered the National Anthem, composed and conducted by his friend Antonio Neumane, who would die a year later, an Ecuadorian citizen himself. He could not have

[198] *El Comercio*, Lima, 24 October 1856.
[199] Archivo General de la Nación, Defunciones 1889, 279/140.

imagined such a life: born in Senigallia, in the Adriatic coast, a close relative of future Pope Pius IX (Giovanni Ferretti), he performed in several minor Italian theatres during the 1830s, with mostly good reviews. Lanari was his agent, and he performed, for example, on the inauguration of the new theatre of Sansepolcro, in 1836.[200]

In 1840, Ferretti's life took an unexpected turn: he had been hired to perform in Pesaro, but left to join the opera company in Santiago de Cuba. We know this, because he was accused in contemporary Italian newspapers of fleeing from his contracts, and he defended himself with a letter from Marseille, just before his transatlantic departure. Simply put, for him, Cuba was just 'a much more advantageous proposition than Pesaro'.[201] He sang in Santiago de Cuba for a season and then the troupe split in two. One half (Corsini, Gallico and Calvet) went to Puerto Rico; the other half (Neumane, Turri, Zambaiti and Ferretti) went to Kingstown, Jamaica. There, they met Teresa Rossi, who was performing on the island on her return journey to Italy from Peru, her original plan being to go home after two years in Lima with the Pantanellis. Rossi knew Zambaiti from her time in Italy: they both had sung together at least once, in Sampierdarena in 1834.[202] Together, the five of them decided to try their luck in the Andes, starting in Ecuador.[203]

Even in 1846, in a letter from his sister, she was still assuming that Paolo was coming back home at some point.[204] She could never have imagined that his brother was going to die in another continent, in a small town in Peru, after being such a key figure in the promotion of Italian opera in so many different cities thousands of miles from Italy. And neither could Ferretti. So many others also stayed in the Andes after the 1840s, never to return to Europe, including the Pantanellis themselves. From travelling artists, they became immigrants. And while one would think of Italians singers in the Americas primarily as part of a global operatic market, hired by impresarios and agents for regular seasons, these lives stretch and that image to its limits. And in those limits, circumstances transformed the lives of those who decided to try their fortunes in one of the most remote, and most novel, of contemporary operatic markets.

For many singers, the Andean region, like other operatic scenes far from Italy, served as a chance to earn money and recognition that could only be dreamed of for the Italian operatic scene. Clorinda Corradi, and Teresa Rossi, in particular, became epoch-making stars: they seemed to have been truly talented

---

[200] *Teatri, arti e letteratura*, Bologna, 14 July 1836.
[201] *Teatri, arti e letteratura*, Bologna, 24 December 1840.
[202] *Il Censore universale dei teatri*, Milan, 1 November 1834.
[203] *Allgemeine Musikalische Zeitung*, Leipzig, 17 May 1843.
[204] Izquierdo, 'For a Moment, I Felt Like I was Back in Italy', 138.

singers, by all standards. For example, Paulin Niboyet, who came from France where she had heard many famous European singers, praised them both in her journal of Chile and Peru in the late 1840s. In her own words, most Italian singers in the region 'executed' the operas they performed, 'and god knows the word to execute was never more profoundly true'.[205] In contrast, her opinion was that Pantanelli and Rossi (the first small and strong, the second tall and thin) were 'queens' in their technique, 'charming in elegance, grace, and style'.[206] Johann Jakob von Tschudi, in a similar vein, considered that by all measures 'Signora Pantanelli is an excellent singer, and would be heard with pleasure even in Europe. Some other members of the company have middling talents, but the rest are decidedly bad'.[207]

But even so, great singers as they were, the level of adoration that Pantanelli and Rossi felt in the Andes was probably outside anything they could have expected in Italy, where they would only have just another great singer in the most competitive of markets. The poems written for and about them in South America, in Italian as well as in Spanish, if compiled, could certainly fill a small book. Some of those poems were decidedly bad, as was often the case at the time, but there are also some really great ones. For example, there is the short poem *For the Album of Teresa Rossi*, written by the celebrated Venezuelan writer and intellectual Andrés Bello, who tries to imagine how it might feel for Rossi to be a singer 'standing on foreign lands, crossing expansive oceans', opening meaningful layers of her own experience rather than standard verses of praise.[208]

Singers that were in the mid or the lower tiers of the operatic business in Italy could easily become major stars abroad. That might explain why so many singers hired for one or two years ended up staying for so long, or for life, in the Andean region. Of course, not everyone was Teresa Rossi or Clorinda Corradi-Pantanelli, and that is exactly the point. Even Teresa Rossi had a much different training from Clorinda Corradi: while performing as equals in Peru or Chile, Corradi had had a long and distinguished career as a performer before crossing the Atlantic, having sung in all the major Italian theatres, and alongside major stars of the period, even premiering a trouser role written for her by Donizetti.[209] Rossi, on the other hand, had just started her career when she left for Cuba. She grew up as a singer in Cuba, and for her, like for many

[205] Paulin Niboyet, *Les mondes nouveaux: Voyage Anecdotique dans L'Océan Pacifique* (J. Renouard et cie, 1854), 170.

[206] Niboyet, *Les mondes nouveaux*, 170.   [207] Tschudi, *Peru: Reiseskizzen*, 84–5.

[208] Andrés Bello, *Obras Completas de don Andrés Bello. Volumen III: Poesías* (Pedro Ramírez, 1883), 331.

[209] Paola Ciarlantini, 'Il percorso biografico-artistico di Clorinda Corradi Pantanelli, "musa" di Carlo Leopardi', in *Atti del Convegno 'Cantante di Marca'* (Associazione Marchigiana per la Ricerca, 2010), 77.

other singers, the Andean region served as a less competitive arena, where audiences knew much less about Italian opera and trained voices.

The problem of evaluating the quality of singers and performances was an acute one. Take the case of Vincenzo Zapucci: he was widely considered a star in Chile, Ecuador and Peru in the 1820s and 1830s, but when he came back in 1840, alongside the Pantanellis, he was hissed by the audience, which now could compare him to truly professional singers.[210] In 1832, the Limenian politician Felipe Pardo, who had been in Europe for some time, complained in a letter to his mother, who lived in Arequipa, about the local audience, who, according to him, could not tell the difference between good and bad singers: 'The audience cheers everyone the same. Poor devils, they haven't seen anything else, so everything seems like a marvel to them.'[211] But years later, the same Pardo would concede that Rossi and Corradi were indeed different from the rest of the pack. For him, the 1840 company was only about those two singers, the rest being something less than supporting characters. Pantanelli and Rossi, he writes, 'are not part of that general mass of *donnas* with which Italy provides the musical markets of the globe'.[212]

We must also consider that many singers arrived in the Andean region not as part of a company, but for personal or practical reasons, and for whom joining an opera company came only as an afterthought. Juditta Ricci, for example, came from Brazil (and probably Argentina), but only stayed for a short while in Chile as a soloist soprano before disappearing from the record. Or Henry Lanza, son of the celebrated London-based teacher Gesualdo Lanza, who came to Chile in 1840 to serve as chapelmaster in the cathedral and as a singing teacher to rich families. In a private letter a few months after her arrival in Chile, in 1844, Clorinda Corradi was deeply impressed by how Lanza, or his friend Enrico Maffei, could have had so much success as teachers and singers, when, according to her, their technique and their voice were so poor that they could hardly sing in a room larger than a salon.[213]

Beyond Corradi and Rossi, there were also plenty of other competing *donnas* in this market. Idalide Turri, wife of Antonio Neumane, often performed alongside her husband. However, she was often criticized for the volume of her voice, a better fit for soirees than the theatre, according to contemporary reviews.[214] Indeed, her previous career in Italy had been as a *dilettante*.

---

[210] *El Comercio*, Lima, 12 December 1840.

[211] Museo Pedro de Osma, Felipe Pardo collection, letter from 28 April 1832.

[212] Pardo y Aliaga, *Poesías y escritos*, 346.

[213] Letter from Clorinda Corradi, 15 July 1844. In Richert, 'La correspondencia del pintor alemán', 153.

[214] *El Comercio*, Lima, 13 May 1848.

Teresa Pusterla, wife of tenor Gaetano Bastoggi, often performed alongside Rossi and Pantanelli in friendly soirees, rather than in the theatre.[215] The only serious competition to Rossi and Pantanelli was Lucrezia Micciarelli. She was hired by Antonio Neumane, as representative of the theatre manager in Lima, Francisco Coya, with Alberto Torri serving as her agent in Italy. Her contract included a monthly allowance of 400 pesos (more than a yearly salary for many musicians and actors at the time), plus two benefit concerts a year, and the cost of the journey.[216] Heinrich Witt, in his private diary of his life in Lima, wrote about the hotly contested debates between those that still loved Teresa Rossi as 'their' prima donna, and those who now favoured Micciarelli, particularly as Elvira in *Ernani*.[217]

Micciarelli's time in Peru also shows the difficult circumstances singers, particularly female singers, had to endure while abroad. Part of her contract was not fulfilled after her arrival, and she had to endure a long legal case against Coya in the courts.[218] Coya, with the help of a Chilean technician working in the theatre, purportedly tried to kill her by cutting the support for the scenery while she was performing *Linda di Chamounix'*.[219] And a few weeks after her arrival, she was accused of leaving her husband to elope with Antonio Neumane, her lover.[220] In a long letter published by the local newspaper, she explained the situation: a daring gesture considering how conservative Lima was. She had applied for divorce, her husband was a violent man – he had attacked her in public with a knife – and lived off of from her income.[221] Newspapers also concocted a rivalry between her and Rossi, to the point both of them publish a statement of their 'friendship and mutual consideration', asking to 'please stop [goading] us to attack the other, since we are both sensible to our mutual feelings'.[222] However, in private, Rossi was scared of Micciarelli: she was younger, very good in the new repertoire (like Verdi's *Ernani*), and had a unique technique Rossi had never heard before. Listening to Micciarelli, Rossi felt that while she was still singing the same works in the Andes, technique and repertoire might have completely changed back home.[223]

If life could be difficult for Italian singers, it was no easier for local artists. There were at least two prominent Peruvian sopranos working in the 1840s: Dolores Cuevas and María España. Lima had a long tradition of local singers, trained in the tradition of Spanish *tonadilla*, like Rosa Merino (who premiered the national anthem of Peru in 1821), and Micaela Villegas, *La Perricholi*,

---

[215] *El Comercio*, Lima, 19 September 1848.   [216] Archivo General de la Nación, RPJ428.

[217] Witt, *The Diary of Heinrich Witt*, IV/164.   [218] Archivo General de la Nación, RPJ428.

[219] Moncloa, *Diccionario Teatral del Perú*, 102.   [220] *El Comercio*, Lima, 29 April 1848.

[221] *El Comercio*, Lima, 27 April 1848.   [222] *El Comercio*, Lima, 12 December 1848.

[223] Letter from Teresa Rossi to Isidora Zegers, 12 December 1848. Archivo Central Andrés Bello.

mistress of the viceroy and the subject of films, novels and an operetta by Offenbach. Dolores Cuevas jumped from private soirees to the theatre when she was hired by Francisco Coya to help with the opera season in 1848. She sang alongside Micciarelli, who, according to the newspaper, helped and trained the newcomer.[224] Audiences gave the Lima-born singer an ovation on her first night.[225] She performed in Lima between 1848 and 1851, the year she disappeared. Notices were published searching for her, with a reward being offered, but no one found her.[226]

Dolores Cuevas sang alongside María España, and Paolo Ferretti, in one of the most important operatic performances of the decade: the Western Hemisphere premiere of Verdi's *Alzira* in Lima, in January of 1850.[227] Cuevas played Zuma, while María España embodied Alzira, the Inca princess, and Paolo Ferretti played Guzmano, the Spanish soldier. The opera was premiered for María España's benefit, who, in a long letter in the newspaper, dedicates the performance to Lima, her city: 'where I was born and where my lyrical training has been developed'.[228] The performance might be seen as a consecration for María España. She sang for the first time in the theatre of Lima in June 1840, a few weeks before the unexpected arrival of the Pantanelli company that would also change her life.[229] She travelled extensively together with her husband Ferretti, from Quito in the north to Concepción in the south, returning to Lima only in 1861, a star and a local hero, working as a singing teacher until her death on October 10, 1877.[230]

Alessandro Zambaiti also became a household name. According to Clorinda Corradi, he was an excellent singer, but often affected by vocal problems and some unknown sickness, which doomed his career.[231] Rossi also considered him a good tenor, much better than others in the region, particularly in Bellini and Donizetti.[232] Innocenzo Pellegrini gained prominence as a teacher after a short run as opera singer. He arrived in Lima with the company of 1848, premiering as the protagonist of Verdi's *Ernani*. After his two-year contract in Lima ran out in 1850, he and his wife Rosina Mauri organized a company to perform opera in California, then in the middle of a gold rush. Their company was touted in San Francisco as the 'most distinguished vocal performers of the

---

[224] *El Comercio*, Lima, 18 September 1848.   [225] *El Comercio*, Lima, 27 September 1848.

[226] *El Comercio*, Lima, 12 August 1851/28 April 1852.

[227] *El Comercio*, Lima, 18 January 1850.   [228] *El Comercio*, Lima, 18 January 1850.

[229] *El Comercio*, Lima, 26 June 1840.

[230] Carlos Raygada, *Guía musical del Perú* (Fénix, 1856), 25.

[231] Letter from Clorinda Corradi, 13 April 1844. In Richert, 'La correspondencia del pintor alemán', 153.

[232] Letter from Teresa Rossi to Isidora Zegers, 12 December 1848. Archivo Central Andrés Bello.

lyric companies of Peru and Chile'.[233] Together with Angelo Francia and James Weitz, they performed *La sonnambula*, the first complete opera in San Francisco.[234] He returned to Chile in 1855, but on his way back, he stopped in Mexico, where he wrote an early national anthem premiered in the Teatro Nacional.[235] In Chile, he became a respected teacher, a member of the Universidad de Chile, and in 1860 he founded the new *Sociedad Filarmónica* in Santiago. He was also a respected composer of salon music, and at least nine of his works survive today, including a waltz on themes from *La Traviata*.

Locals often begged singers not to leave, pleading their case in print during the waning days of any operatic season. That was the case when the Pantanellis were thinking about leaving Lima for the first time, in 1842,[236] or when they finally decided to go to Chile two years later.[237] But that was not always the case, and even Teresa Rossi and Clorinda Corradi were, after a decade performing in the Andes, considered rather old-fashioned: 'always the same trills and the same repertoire', as one reviewer put it in Lima in 1848.[238] Others put it more bluntly: that it was difficult to hear old singers, now 'beyond their fifties', when people wanted new faces, new voices, new sounds.[239]

Finally, it is important to consider that, while performing in the Andes could mean fame and money for Italian singers, there were also important dangers to consider when travelling so far from home. There was always the danger of fraud, of not receiving the money that had been promised beforehand in Italy, as it happened to Micciarelli in 1848. And there also was the danger of a failed season, which could lead to a lack of resources for the return journey of the singers. This was a well-known danger, enough so to be discussed in *L'Italia Musicale*: 'We received news from the theatre in Lima, South America. The season was a failure and those poor singers now have to find a way to finance their journey back home. Living in such a small city on such a faraway coast, they now give concerts to improve their luck.'[240]

But perhaps the greatest danger was to personal safety, with robberies, assaults, disappearance and disease. This has been often recognized as one of the key factors affecting decisions to travel and perform in the Americas at this time, particularly after the death of Henriette Sontag from cholera in

---

[233] George Martin, *Verdi at the Golden Gate: Opera and San Francisco in the Gold Rush Years* (University of California Press, 1993), 23.

[234] Peter Mancall, *American Eras: Westward Expansion, 1800–1860* (Gale, 1999), 53.

[235] Gerónimo Baqueiro, *Historia de la música en México: La música en el period independiente* (Instituto Nacional de Bellas Artes, 1964), 563.

[236] *El Comercio*, Lima, 18 January 1842.   [237] *El Comercio*, Lima, 2 March 1844.

[238] *El Comercio*, Lima, 28 December 1848.   [239] *El Comercio*, Lima, 4 August 1852.

[240] *L'Italia Musicale*, Milan, 6 March 1850.

Mexico in 1854.[241] Something similar happened during the 1842 opera season in Guayaquil, Ecuador. The company led by Antonio Neumane arrived in Guayaquil during the first week of September, and very quickly Juan Pablo Izquieta, the local manager, organized a short season.[242] The operas were performed with piano accompaniment, since there was no orchestra in Guayaquil, and the repertoire included *Norma*, *Barbiere*, *Sonnambula*, *Elissir*, *Marino Faliero* and *Belisario*.[243] The fervour, as usual, included long articles on the company and a new poem for Teresa Rossi: 'Quella voce, quell' accento'.[244]

The same day that poem for Rossi was published, the local newspaper printed the news about some unknown fever that had been detected 'among some individuals' in the city. Two weeks later, all public gatherings and entertainment had been cancelled.[245] It is quite probable that the celebrations for Independence Day that same evening, with a packed theatre listening to the opera company performing patriotic songs and opera arias, was central in the expansion of the disease, later recognized as yellow fever. By early November, more than forty people were dying each day in a city of less than 20,000 people.[246] The actual number of people who died at the time is unknown, but it was more than 10 per cent of the local population. The singers, led by Neumane, fled to El Morro, a little town outside Guayaquil, and survived. But it took decades for opera to overcome the trauma and return to Guayaquil. Helpless and unable to escape the region, during those isolated weeks Neumane built the connections to stay and make a life in Ecuador as a music teacher. The rest of the singers went further down the coast to Peru, to join the Pantanellis and form a new company in Lima.

To sum up, singers who performed in the Andes during the 1840s, of which I have tried to portray different lives and outcomes, were not travelling artists performing a well-trodden repertoire to a mostly passive audience. They had to overcome dangers, educate their listeners and accommodate local tastes. And local circumstances, the people they met and the material and social realities they got to know shaped their lives, careers and the lives of many others. Many of them became migrants, unknowingly creating cluster migrations that would be deeply important for local cultural scenes, as well as to the expansion of Italian culture and language in the Andean region more generally. And beyond

---

[241] Walter, *Oper: Geschichte einer Institution*, 53.

[242] Biblioteca Municipal de Guayaquil, Documentos de Policía, 12 September 1842.

[243] Huerta, *Guayaquil en 1842*, 28.

[244] *Correo Semanal de Guayaquil*, Guayaquil, 9 October 1842.

[245] *Correo Semanal de Guayaquil*, Guayaquil, 23 October 1842.

[246] Huerta, *Guayaquil en 1842*, 24.

opera, they were central agents in this period of radical changes for Andean societies, in transit from colonial to independent attitudes that were still in a formative process. As the portrait of Clorinda Pantanelli in the National History Museum of Chile exemplifies, unknowingly, Italian opera artists even went on to define at least part of the national and cultural identity of several Andean nations.

Epilogue: The Long Impact of Opera

In 1853, during an opera performance, unknown revolutionaries flooded the theatre of Lima with leaflets inciting a revolution against the authorities. The owners of the theatre, including Charles Zuderell, were restrained, accused of subversion.[247] The event, well known in Peruvian history, symbolizes how ingrained theatrical life, and Italian opera in particular, had become in the cultural and social landscape of the largest Andean cities, particularly in Lima, Santiago and Valparaiso. That moment represents how opera performances had become a relevant public space in the Andean region, significant enough to dare throwing those pamphlets. By the early 1850s, Italian opera was part of a shared culture, enough so for a politician to say that he wished the Peruvian parliament to die 'as Violetta does in *Traviata*: Oh God! To die so young?' knowing the reference would be easily recognized by fellow readers.[248] Or how, in 1866, Manuel Atanasio Fuentes, in his celebrated *Sketches of Lima*, could describe the difference between life in the capital and the provinces through the story of a donkey, Laureano, who, upon returning to rural life after years of working in Lima, brayed in sadness, remembering the 'melancholic strains of Bellini', and having 'no longer, as in Lima, the sonority, harmony and vigour of the creations of Rossini or Mozart'.[249]

Italian opera had come a long way, now a recognized symbol of modern urban life. A decade after it first arrived in the region, Italian opera permeated everything, from popular music, to Catholic church music, to military bands, to national anthems; so much so that even music composed before this period was often rearranged, in churches and the stage, to fit with the new vocal and stylistic preferences imprinted by Italian opera. Even national anthems came to be defined by some of these artists, as in the cases of Ecuador and Bolivia. By the 1850s, an important part of the music composed and printed in Peru and Chile at that time consisted of fantasias and variations on themes from Donizetti, Bellini and Verdi, including at least four by Federico Guzmán, the most celebrated local pianist in the Andes at that time.

Opera also made a huge impact in other forms of artistic production, from paintings to architecture, and also, of course, in the transformation of the

---

[247] Alfonso Quiroz, *La deuda defraudada: Consolidación de 1850 y dominio económico en el Perú* (Instituto Nacional de Cultura, 1987), 125.

[248] *El Comercio*, Lima, 14 May 1857.

[249] Fuentes, *Lima: Or, Sketches of the Capital of Peru*, 184.

musical style of local composers.[250] For example, the premiere of Verdi's *Alzira* in 1850, with María España in the title role, had an enormous impact in the dramatic production of an entire generation of young Peruvian writers.[251] And, as I mentioned before, proposals for new operas, at least in terms of libretti, were also common. There was also the use of opera as a symbol in literary works. In 1859, for example, a new play in La Paz, *Don Manuel*, was written in the form of a fake opera libretto, signed under the guise of 'La Ballini'. It is a play in two acts criticizing contemporary politics and politicians, with choirs of 'deaf, blinds, mutes' contrasting with the very bureaucratic *recitativo* discourses of Don Manuel, the politician (most probably a caricature of Manuel Hermenegildo Guerra).[252] Juan Rodríguez Gutiérrez, the celebrated Ecuadorian author, also used opera as the framework for one of his earliest plays, *Bellini*, published and premiered in 1862 in Guayaquil. The play, loosely based on Bellini's life, combines certain biographical elements with the plot of *I Capuleti*, with Bellini portrayed more as a symbol of Italian opera than a real person.[253]

Opera completely changed the art of criticism in local newspapers. Before Italian opera, reviews were sparse, dedicated to very special events. During the 1840s, they became commonplace, and readers complained when, after the opera season finished, newspapers stopped publishing them, having become accustomed to their combination of entertainment, gossip and education.[254] Opera also comes forward in the writings of many of the most important authors from the period, many of whom wrote reviews on the subject, from long essays (like those by Felipe Pardo y Aliaga) to some of the most conspicuous poetry (like that of Andrés Bello). Opera also features prominently in personal writings, like letters and diaries, as well as in the fictional literature of the period.[255] As I have mentioned before, even *Facundo*, Domingo Faustino Sarmiento's essay that would become one of the defining works of nineteenth-century Latin American literature and intellectual history, was shaped by his experience of the Pantanelli company in the mid-1840s.

Many of those involved in the opera business who, for different reasons, decided to stay in the Andes, had a large impact in the development of local musical life. Giovanni Bayetti, who arrived with an opera company in 1853,

---

[250] José Manuel Izquierdo, 'Rossinian Opera in Translation: José Bernardo Alzedo's Church Music in Mid-Nineteenth-Century Chile', *The Opera Quarterly* 35/4 (2019), 251–75.

[251] Rubén Vargas Ugarte, *Historia General del Perú* (C. Mila Batres, 1966), Volume 9/58.

[252] *Don Manuel: Ópera Bufo-Seria en dos Actos* (Imprenta Paceña, 1859).

[253] Juan Rodríguez Gutiérrez, *Teatro Ecuatoriano. Bellini* (Imprenta de Rafael Arias, 1862).

[254] Aguayo, 'Gran función lírica'.

[255] Carmen Peña, 'El piano de Leonor: Una mirada a la interpretación musical de la heroína de Martín Rivas', *Resonancias* 15/26 (2010), 21–39.

became the first singing teacher in Chile's National Conservatoire. He would be substituted in 1859 by Innocenzo Pellegrini, who arrived with Micciarelli in 1848. And Clorinda Corradi herself would become a teacher there from 1861 to 1875.[256] Innocente Ricordi, son of Giovanni Ricordi, who arrived with the opera company that same year of 1848, marrying a local, Juliana Villavicencia, a year after. In Lima he opened a branch of his family's business in Lima, the first dedicated music store in the Andean region. He sent local music to be printed back in Italy, including the first set of scores of national dances of Peru that we know of,[257] and he imported large quantities of vocal scores that his father and then his brother, could provide: 'all the most famous and modern operas, performed in theatres in Europe (Paris, London, Vienna, etc.) as well as those performed and not yet performed in our theatre in Lima' could be found there.[258] The opening of his store was, like opera, greeted as a sign of how 'Lima is walking the road of civilization'.[259] And Ricordi always announced when people could buy 'the opera that is being performed today in the theatre', whether for 'voice and piano, solo piano, piano 4 hands, or variations'.[260]

Most intriguing is that, beyond the economic, cultural and social networks of the 1840s, the impact of Italian opera, projected from those decades, can also be felt today. First and foremost, and perhaps most strikingly, by the sheer power of opera on the urban landscape of cities like La Paz and Santiago, where both Teatro Municipal buildings are classified as heritage sites. These venues are today central features of their respective cities, and the same can be said of other regional theatres from this period that have survived until our days, like the much-transformed *Teatro Principal* in Lima, or the 1870 *Teatro Municipal* in Tacna. Many others have, sadly, disappeared in this earthquake-prone part of the globe.

The memory of opera as a symbol of that period, and its dichotomies, is also alive in contemporary arts. For example, in 2017, Ana Luz Ormazábal created a satirical play in Chile about the Pantanellis and the first national operas, while in Bolivia Luis Miguel González premiered in 2019 a play about the arrival of conductor and composer Leopoldo Vincenti in 1845 and the beginnings of Italian opera.[261] Even more astounding is the tradition to celebrate national holidays with opera. In Chile, for example, the president always attends an

---

[256] Luis Sandoval, *Reseña histórica del Conservatorio Nacional de Música y Declamación: 1849 a 1911* (Imprenta Gutenberg, 1911), 12.

[257] *Zamacueca: Baile Nacional del Perú para Piano Forte* (Inocente Ricordi, [1849]).

[258] *El Comercio*, Lima, 1 August 1848.   [259] *El Comercio*, Lima, 24 August 1848.

[260] *El Comercio*, Lima, 9 September 1848.

[261] González play is titled 'El Himnovador', and premiered in La Paz in 2018. Ana Luz Ormazábal premiered her play 'Opera' in 2016.

opera on the night of Independence Day, the most important artistic gala of the year, and one of the only three traditional acts celebrated by the president on that day, apart from the Catholic Te Deum and the military parade.

Thus, the impact of Italian opera in Latin American culture has been enormous, and goes well beyond the most recognizable scenes of the Atlantic coast: those of Rio de Janeiro/Sao Paulo and Montevideo/Buenos Aires. But what might be less evident is that the earliest moments of Italian opera's reception history in the Andes, during the second quarter of the nineteenth century, were truly in a state of flux. Its success was not self-evident, strategies to make it profitable were multiple, there was much danger and risk for opera companies and singers, and there were active campaigns on the part of audiences, intellectuals and contemporary local artists to either make it work or fail. Given how successful Italian opera would become for Latin American urban audiences during the second half of the century, it would be easy to take its success for granted. But, as many singers and impresarios noticed, this was a new frontier, one which had only received, until then, sporadic, episodic, almost comet-like visits from Italian opera singers. Opera became the symbol of civilization and modernity. But also, perhaps because of that same reason, it was deeply contested by local performing artists, who had to cope with its overwhelming impact on the cultural scene. Many of those who came to sing in the 1840s became locals, recasting themselves as teachers or using their fortune to foster new businesses, becoming part of local society, their families as Chilean, Peruvian or Ecuadorian as Italian.

But we cannot deny that, at the same time, Italian opera was, undeniably, a colonial-imperialist force of its own, forcing certain readings of what is and what is not culture and the arts. Most probably, from the private sources we have, most of the Italian singers themselves believed that Italian opera was a more civilized form of culture than any local performative practice. And their sheer influence reshaped the expectations people had over artists, in particular of professional singers. As José Zapiola wrote at the time, with Italian opera people started to make a difference between 'a *cantatriz*, a singer who can sing with all the rules and grace of art; and a *cantora*, who can only have a modest intelligence and knowledge of the rules'.[262] Many forms of popular culture, which until then had had a safe place in the theatre, were shunted to the side, with significant consequences for musicians and actors' jobs and status, in that difficult transition from colonial to republican governments.

By the 1860s, Italian opera had been firmly established as a regular part of performing seasons. There were travelling troupes, arranging their contracts in

---

[262] *Semanario Musical Chileno*, Santiago, 24 April 1852.

every port, but also Italian companies hired to provide for opera seasons regularly, every two or three years, as had been the case since the mid-1840s. These Italian companies were often supplemented by singers from Brazil or Argentina, but also from California or Australia, creating a broader Asia-Pacific operatic scene with its own repertoires and mechanisms. All of this endured until the early twentieth century, when the opening of the Panama Canal, the independence of Cuba and the beginning of the Great War completely reshaped maritime networks, routes and the movement of people inside Latin America as well as in its connections to the Atlantic and the Pacific.

Examining the first years of this process provides us with tools to go beyond the frameworks we have inherited in studying global opera during this period. From the perspective of Latin American music scholarship, the idea of operatic history as an uncritical succession of names, dates and performances grounded on newspaper sources. From contemporary opera scholarship, the understanding of operatic reception as a passive form of history, in which the only agency is carried out by Italian opera itself, in a rather abstract way. As I have shown, creating a new operatic scene, with its own audience, mechanisms and networks, was not an easy task. But it was possible, and this exploration of some of those possibilities, why they worked (or not) and the journeys of those involved in them allows us to go beyond the epistemological limits of opera imagined in colonial terms: as a European artefact to be consumed, uncritically, by an abstract global otherness. The triumph of Italian opera as a global phenomenon in the mid-nineteenth century cannot be considered a self-fulling prophecy, and a nuanced history of its reception needs to acknowledge the intricacies and central role of agencies, appropriations and the transformation of the genre itself according to specific local needs, as well as specific material, cultural and social realities.

References

Archives

Archivo Central Andrés Bello (Santiago)
Archivo Histórico del Guayas (Guayaquil)
Archivo Nacional de Chile (Santiago)
Archivo Republicano, Archivo Histórico Nacional (Lima)
Archivo y Biblioteca Nacionales de Bolivia (Sucre)
Biblioteca Marciana (Venecia)
Biblioteca Municipal de Guayaquil (Guayaquil)
Biblioteca Nacional de Chile (Santiago)
Biblioteca Nacional del Perú (Lima)
Biblioteca Nazionale Centrale (Florence)
Centro Cultural Biblioteca Ecuatoriana Aurelio Espinosa Pólit (Quito)
Conservatorio di Musica Giuseppe Verdi (Milan)
Museo de Arte de Lima (Lima)
Museo Pedro de Osma (Lima)

Newspapers and Periodicals

Allgemeine Musikalische Zeitung (Leipzig)
Bazar di novita artistiche (Milan)
Correo Semanal de Guayaquil (Guayaquil)
Corriere degli Spettacoli Italiani (Bologna)
Crónica del Teatro (Quito)
El Amigo del Pueblo (Lima)
El Araucano (Santiago)
El Comercio (Lima)
El Investigador (Lima)
El Mercurio (Santiago)
El Mercurio de Valparaíso (Valparaíso)
El Mercurio Peruano (Lima)
El Peruano (Lima)
El Progreso (Santiago)
El Telégrafo (Lima)
Gazeta Extraordinaria Ministerial (Santiago)
Gazetta Musicale di Milano (Milan)
Il Censore universale dei teatri (Milan)
Il Pirata (Milan)
L'Italia Musicale (Milan)

La Época (La Paz)
Semanario Musical Chileno (Santiago)
Teatri, arti e letteratura (Bologna)

Bibliography

Agid, Philippe and Jean-Claude Tarondeau. *The Management of Opera: An International Comparative Study* (Palgrave Macmillan, 2010).

Aguayo, Macarena. 'Gran función lírica, con los mejores trozos de las óperas modernas: El consumo de la ópera en La Paz durante la Temporada de la compañía Ferreti (1847)', unpublished BA thesis, Pontificia Universidad Católica de Chile (2019).

Amunátegui, Miguel Luis. *Las primeras representaciones dramáticas en Chile* (Imprenta Nacional, 1888).

Angelelli, Pedro. *Habiendo llegado a nuestras manos [. . .]* (Imprenta de los Huérfanos, 1812).

Arago, Jacques. *Deux Océans* (Kiessling, Schnée et Cie., 1954).

Arteaga, Domingo. 'La representación dramática que subió al primer grado de esplendor' (Unknown document published in 1827).

Aspden, Suzanne. *Operatic Geographies: The Place of Opera and the Opera House* (University of Chicago Press, 2019).

Bailey, Candace. *Unbinding Gentility: Women Making Music in the Nineteenth-Century South* (University of Illinois Press, 2021).

Baqueiro, Gerónimo. *Historia de la música en México: La música en el period independiente* (Instituto Nacional de Bellas Artes, 1964).

Bello, Andrés. *Obras Completas de don Andrés Bello. Volumen III: Poesías* (Pedro Ramírez, 1883).

Bentley, Charlotte. 'Resituating Transatlantic Opera: The Case of the Théâtre d'Orléans, New Orleans, 1819–1859', unpublished PhD thesis, University of Cambridge (2017).

Bonelli, Hugh de. *Travels in Bolivia: With a Tour Across the Pampas to Buenos Ayres* (Hurst and Blackett, 1854).

Bowen, Michael. 'Distraer y gobernar: Teatro y diversiones públicas en Santiago de Chile durante la era de las revoluciones (1780–1836)', *Historia* 49/1 (2016), 27–56.

Bravo, Álvaro and José Manuel Izquierdo. *Antonio Neumane: Antología para Canto y Piano* (Ediciones A/B, 2020).

Capelán, Montserrat. 'La tonadilla escénica en Venezuela o el proceso de criollización de un género hispano', *Anuario Musical* 72 (2017), 137–52.

Carilla, Emilio. 'Revisión de Olmedo', *Thesaurus* 19/1 (1964), 129–46.

Cavieres, Eduardo. 'Estructura y funcionamiento de las sociedades comerciales de Valparaiso durante el siglo XIX (1820–1880)', *Cuadernos de Historia* 4 (1984), 61–86.

Ciarlantini, Paola. 'Il percorso biografico-artistico di Clorinda Corradi Pantanelli, "musa" di Carlo Leopardi', in *Atti del Convegno 'Cantante di Marca'* (Associazione Marchigiana per la Ricerca, 2010), 77.

Collard, Ian. *Pacific Steam Navigation Company: Fleet List & History* (Amberley, 2014).

Dávalos, Ricardo. *Lima de antaño: cuentos y tradiciones, críticas literarias, artículos de costumbres y de índole narrativa* (Montaner y Simón, 1925).

Don Manuel: Ópera Bufo-Seria en dos Actos (Imprenta Paceña, 1859).

Estenssoro, Juan Carlos. 'La Plebe Ilustrada: El Pueblo en las Fronteras de la Razón', in Charles Walker (ed.), *Entre la retórica y la insurgencia: Las ideas y los movimientos sociales en los Andes, siglo XVIII* (Centro Bartolomé de las Casas, 1995), 257–77.

Everist, Mark. *The Empire at the Opéra: Theatre, Power and Music in Second Empire Paris* (Cambridge University Press, 2021).

Fuentes, Manuel. *Lima: Or, Sketches of the Capital of Peru* (Trübern, 1866).

Garriga, José. *Continuación y suplemento del Prontuario de don Severo Aguirre* (Librería de don Valentín Francés, 1802).

Giacometti, Diana. 'La figura dell'impresario musicale: Walter Mocchi e la costruzione di un'undistria operistica fra Italia e Sud America', unpublished PhD thesis, Università Ca' Foscari Venezia (2013).

Gutiérrez, Juan Rodríguez. *Teatro Ecuatoriano: Bellini* (Imprenta de Rafael Arias, 1862).

Hall, Basil. *Extracts from a Journal: Written on the Coasts of Chili, Peru and Mexico, in the Years 1820, 1821 and 1822* (A. Constable, 1826).

Huerta, Pedro José. *Guayaquil en 1842: Rocafuerte y la epidemia de la fiebre amarilla* (Editorial de la Universidad de Guayaquil, 1987).

Izquierdo, José Manuel. 'Totaleindruck o impresión total: La Telésfora de Aquinas Ried como proyecto político, creación literario-musical, reflejo personal y encuentro con el otro', *Revista Musical Chilena* 65/215 (2011), 5–22.

Izquierdo, José Manuel. 'El Militar Retirado de Pedro Ximénez Abrill (Arequipa, 1784 – Sucre, 1856): Una tonadilla inedita en el Perú independiente', *Diagonal: An Ibero-American Music Review* 1/2 (2016).

Izquierdo, José Manuel. 'Rossini's Reception in Latin America: Scarcity and Imagination in Two Early Chilean Sources', in Ilaria Narici, Emilio Sala, Emanuele Senici and Benjamin Walton (eds.), *Gioachino Rossini 1868–2018* (Fondazione Rossini, 2018), 413–36.

Izquierdo, José Manuel. 'Rossinian Opera in Translation: José Bernardo Alzedo's Church Music in Mid-Nineteenth-Century Chile', *The Opera Quarterly* 35/4 (2019), 251–75.

Izquierdo, José Manuel. '"For a Moment, I Felt Like I was Back in Italy": Early South American Experiences of Italian Opera Singers (1840–1860)', in Axel Körner and Paulo Kühl (eds.), *Italian Opera in Global and Transnational Perspective: Reimagining Italianità in the Long Nineteenth Century* (Cambridge University Press, 2021), 133–46.

Izquierdo, José Manuel. 'The Invention of an Opera House: The 1844 Teatro Victoria in Valparaiso, Chile', *Cambridge Opera Journal* 32/2 (2021), 129–53.

Izquierdo, José Manuel and Victor Rondon. 'Las canciones patrióticas de José Bernardo Alzedo (1788–1878)', *Revista Musical Chilena* 68/222 (2014), 12–34.

Izquierdo Castañeda, Jorge. 'El desaparecido teatro de Lambayeque', *Semanario Clarín Chiclayo*, 5 November 2017. http://semanarioclarin-chiclayo.blogspot.com/2017/11/el-desaparecido-treatro-de-lambayeque.html (Revised 16 March 2022).

Klein, Alexander. *El sastre de dos mundos: Luigi Bazzani y la ópera en América* (Universidad de Los Andes, 2022).

Kühl, Paulo and Axel Körner. *Italian Opera in Global and Transnational Perspective: Reimagining Italianità in the Long Nineteenth Century* (Cambridge University Press, 2022).

Lamus, Mariana. *Pintores en el escenario teatral* (Universidad del Rosario, 2014).

Le Guin, Elisabeth. *The Tonadilla in Performance: Lyric Comedy in Enlightenment Spain* (University of California Press, 2013).

León, Jorge. *Evolución del comercio exterior y del transporte marítimo de Costa Rica 1821–1900* (Editorial Universidad de Costa Rica, 1997).

López, Héctor. *Plaza de Acho: Historia y Tradición* (Fondo Editorial del Congreso del Perú, 2005).

Macera, Pablo. *Teatro Peruano, siglo XIX* (Universidad Nacional Mayor de San Marcos, 1991).

Mancall, Peter. *American Eras: Westward Expansion, 1800–1860* (Gale, 1999).

Martin, George. *Verdi at the Golden Gate: Opera and San Francisco in the Gold Rush Years* (University of California Press, 1993).

Milella, Francesco. 'Este ídolo del mundo músico: Rossini a Città del Messico (1823–1838)', unpublished BA thesis, Università degli Studi di Milano (2016).

Moncloa, Manuel. *Diccionario Teatral del Perú* (Escuela Nacional de Arte Dramático, 2016 [1905]).

Montemorra, Roberta. *Operatic Migrations: Transforming Works and Crossing Boundaries* (Routledge, 2017).

Muñoz, Hugo. 'La recepción discursiva de la figura y obra de Richard Wagner en América Latina durante el siglo XIX', unpublished MA thesis, Pontificia Universidad Católica de Chile (2022).

Niboyet, Paulin. *Les mondes nouveaux: Voyage anecdotique dans L'Océan Pacifique* (J. Renouard et cie, 1854).

Olmedo, José Joaquín. *Obras poéticas de D. José Joaquín Olmedo* (Imprenta Europea, 1848).

Paoletti, Matteo. *A Huge Revolution of Theatrical Commerce: Walter Mocchi and the Italian Musical Theatre Business in South America* (Cambridge University Press, 2020).

Parakilas, James. 'Political Representation and the Chorus in the Nineteenth-Century Opera', *19th-Century Music* 16/2 (1992), 181–202.

Pardo y Aliaga, Felipe. *Poesías y escritos en prosa de don Felipe Pardo* (A. Chaix et cie, 1869).

Peña, Carmen. 'El piano de Leonor: Una mirada a la interpretación musical de la heroína de Martín Rivas', *Resonancias* 15/26 (2010), 21–39.

Pereira Salas, Eugenio. *Historia de la Música en Chile 1850–1900* (Editorial Universitaria, 1950).

Pereira Salas, Eugenio. *Historia del Teatro en Chile: desde sus orígenes hasta la Muerte de Juan Casacuberta* (Ediciones de la Universidad de Chile, 1974).

Polzonetti, Pierpaolo. *Italian Opera in the Age of the American Revolution* (Cambridge University Press, 2011).

Preston, Katherine. *Opera on the Road: Traveling Opera Troupes in the United States, 1825–60* (University of Illinois Press, 1993).

Quiroz, Alfonso. *La deuda defraudada: Consolidación de 1850 y dominio económico en el Perú* (Instituto Nacional de Cultura, 1987).

Radiguet, Max. *Lima y la sociedad peruana* (Biblioteca Nacional del Perú, 1971 [1841]).

Ramón, Emma de. 'Norma y el desacato: la Sociedad chilena frente a la irrupción de las mujeres artistas (1840–1850)', in *Seminario Historia del Arte y Feminismo* (Museo Nacional de Bellas Artes, 2013), 22–39. www.genero.patrimoniocultural.gob.cl/651/articles-49719_archivo_01.pdf.

Reeder, Jessie. *The Forms of Informal Empire: Britain, Latin America, and Nineteenth-Century Literature* (Johns Hopkins University Press, 2020).

Reglamento para los teatros públicos del Perú (Imprenta de E. Aranda, 1849).

Rengifo, David Carlos. 'Le théâtre historique et la construction de la nation: essor, crise et résurgence: Lima 1848–1924', unpublished PhD thesis, Université Rennes 2 (2018).

Riall, Lucy. 'Un "Imperial Meridian" in Peru: Appeal, commercio e scienze dell'imperialismo informale italiano, 1848–1890'. Paper presented in the

X Cantieri di Storia Sissco, Modena, 18–20 September 2019. www.sissco.it/wp-content/uploads/2019/07/Riall-Imperial-Meridian.pdf (Revised March 2022).

Richert, Gertrud. 'La correspondencia del pintor alemán Juan Mauricio Rugendas', *Boletín de la Academia Chilena de la Historia* 19/1 (1952), 91–149.

Ricketts, Mónica. 'El teatro en Lima y la construcción de la nación republicana (1820–1850)', unpublished BA thesis, Pontificia Universidad Católica de Lima (1996).

Rindom, Ditlev. 'Bygone Modernity: Re-imagining Italian Opera in Milan, New York and Buenos Aires, 1887–1914', unpublished PhD thesis, University of Cambridge (2019).

Rodríguez Silva, Andrea. 'Los orígenes del Teatro en Copiapó', unpublished MA thesis, Universidad de Chile (2003).

Rojas, Rolando. *Tiempos de carnaval, el Ascenso de los popular a la cultura nacional, Lima 1822–1922* (Instituto Francés de Estudios Andinos, 2005).

Rojas, Rolando. 'La república imaginada: representaciones culturales y discursos políticos en la independencia peruana (Lima, 1821–1822)', unpublished MA thesis, Universidad Mayor de San Marcos (2009).

Ruschenberger, William. *Three Years in the Pacific: Containing Notices of Brazil, Chile, Bolivia, Peru* (Richard Bentley, 1835).

Rutherford, Susan. 'Crime and Punishment: Tales of the Opera Chorus in Nineteenth-Century Parma', *Nineteenth Century Theatre and Film* 33/2 (2006), 1–11.

Sala, Emilio. *The Sounds of Paris in Verdi's La Traviata* (Cambridge University Press, 2013).

Sánchez, Víctor. *Verdi y España* (Ediciones Akal, 2014).

Sandoval, Luis. *Reseña histórica del Conservatorio Nacional de Música y Declamación: 1849 a 1911* (Imprenta Gutenberg, 1911).

Santos Tornero, José. *Reminiscencias de un Viejo editor* (Imprenta del Mercurio, 1889).

Soux, María Eugenia. 'La música en la ciudad de La Paz, 1845–1885', unpublished BA thesis, Universidad Mayor de San Andrés (1992).

Suárez, Laura. 'Los libretos: un negocio para las imprentas. 1830–1860', in Laura Suárez, ed., *Los Papeles para Euterpe: la Música en la ciudad de México desde la Historia Cultural, siglo XIX* (Instituto de Investigaciones Dr. José María Luis Mora, 2014), 100–42.

The Ruin of Callao, in 1746: An Opera in Three Acts (Oficinas del Comercio, 1847).

Torres, Rondy. 'Tras las huellas armoniosas de una compañía lírica: La Rossi-D'Achiardi en Bogotá', *Revista del Instituto Carlos Vega* 26 (2012), 161–200.

Tschudi, Johann. *Peru: Reiseskizzen aus den Jahrn 1838–1842* (Scheitlin und Zollifoker, 1846).

Vargas Ugarte, Rubén. *Historia General del Perú* (C. Mila Batres, 1966).

Vigueira, Juan Pedro. *'Relajados o reprimidos': Diversiones públicas y vida social en la ciudad de México durante el siglo de las Luces* (Fondo de Cultura Económica, 1987).

Walter, Michael. *Oper: Geschichte einer Institution* (J. B. Metzler, 2016).

Walton, Benjamin. 'Italian Operatic Fantasies in Latin America', *Journal of Modern Italian Studies* 17 (2012), 460–71.

Warren, Robinson. *Dust and Form of Three Oceans and Two Continents* (Charles Scribner, 1859).

Wise, Henry. *Los Gringos, Or an Inside View of Mexico and California, with Wanderings in Peru, Chili and Polynesia* (R. Bentley, 1849).

Witt, Heinrich. *The Diary of Heinrich Witt* (Brill, 2016).

Zamacueca: Baile Nacional del Perú para Piano Forte (Inocente Ricordi, [1849]).

Zapiola, José. *Recuerdos de treinta años* (El Independiente, 1874).

Acknowledgements

It would be impossible for me to thank everyone who supported me on this project. First, of course, the funding from ANID in Chile. This Element was possible thanks to the Fondo Nacional de Desarrollo Científico y Tecnológico, Project numbers 1170265 and 1210151. Benjamin Walton was the one who led me from Latin American music studies to Opera studies, so I am extremely grateful to him, his suggestions and support over the years. Everyone at Tosc@ conferences who gave me ideas, suggestions and support, and to my opera colleagues from South America: Paulo Kühl, Yael Bitrán and Rondy Torres. This Element, in particular, was possible thanks to the help, in so many ways, from Alessandra Jones, Charlotte Bentley and Ditlev Rindom. In my research, I was assisted several times by Macarena Aguayo, Colomba Nomez, Macarena Robledo, Nayive Ananías, Fabian Tobar and Hugo Muñoz. I am extremely grateful for all the support in archives and libraries in Ecuador, Chile, Perú and Bolivia, but I want to give my thanks to Gladys Cisneros, from the Biblioteca Municipal in Guayaquil, and Laura Martínez and Ricardo Rojas, from the Biblioteca Nacional in Lima. Finally, to Bill Everett for his advice and believing in this project.

Cambridge Elements ≡

Elements in Musical Theatre

William A. Everett

University of Missouri–Kansas City

William A. Everett, PhD is Curators' Distinguished Professor of Musicology at the University of Missouri–Kansas City Conservatory, where he teaches courses ranging from medieval music to contemporary musical theatre. His publications include monographs on operetta composers Sigmund Romberg and Rudolf Friml and a history of the Kansas City Philharmonic Orchestra. He is contributing co-editor of the *Cambridge Companion to the Musical* and the *Palgrave Handbook of Musical Theatre Producers*. Current research topics include race, ethnicity and the musical and London musical theatre during the 1890s.

About the Series

Elements in Musical Theatre focus on either some sort of "journey" and its resulting dialogue, or on theoretical issues. Since many musicals follow a quest model (a character goes in search of something), the idea of a journey aligns closely to a core narrative in musical theatre. Journeys can be, for example, geographic (across bodies of water or land masses), temporal (setting musicals in a different time period than the time of its creation), generic (from one genre to another), or personal (characters in search of some sort of fulfilment). Theoretical issues may include topics relevant to the emerging scholarship on musical theatre from a global perspective and can address social, cultural, analytical, and aesthetic perspectives.

Cambridge Elements ≡

Elements in Musical Theatre